Praise for *The Ups.*

Bullying is rife in workplaces across the globe. Instead of just discussing it, or complaining about it, Jessica Hickman set forth to right this wrong and to help businesses create workplace cultures where bullying cannot exist. Her deep care for humanity is as powerful as it is palpable. Read her book, and follow her lead.

John Toomey, Current Global Chair, Workplace Wellness Initiative

Jessica's ability to take a complex topic and make it easier for leaders to digest and implement is so innovative. By the end of the book, I knew exactly how to be proactive rather than reactive, and develop a positive workplace culture for teams to work together and uplift each other. Every leader should read this book and build a generation of upstanders.

Mia Maze, Director/Owner, Mazey Consulting

Standing by while bad things happen to good people is the ultimate absence of leadership. By standing up for being upstanders, not bystanders, Jessica Hickman is walking the talk.

Matt Church, Founder, Thought Leaders; author of *Rise Up: An Evolution in Leadership*

Jess joined Orange City Council's quest for leadership change in 2020 (during the midst of the pandemic) when she designed the Future Focused Leaders program. Jess's Upstander model formed the basis of an extremely successful workforce transformation from which we are still reaping the benefits. I thoroughly recommend this book to all leaders wanting to effect change.

David Waddell, Chief Executive Officer, Orange City Council

What an inspirational and groundbreaking read! *The Upstander Leader* reminds us all that we are the key to transforming workplace culture, and provides leaders with the tools to become genuine upstanders and not just bystanders. It will empower leaders to create change and become champions of workplace culture in their businesses.

Vicki Seccombe, Regional Manager – Western NSW, Business NSW

The Upstander Leader successfully blends the firsthand story of Jessica's own lived experiences with good data and case studies to show the importance of a positive culture in today's workplace and the positive steps we can all take to create such a culture. In an era of fierce competition for talented staff, being equipped to move from bystander to upstander can help you keep your staff and build a business reputation that helps attract new staff.

Scott Hansen, Director General, NSW Department of Primary Industries

THE UPSTANDER LEADER

THE

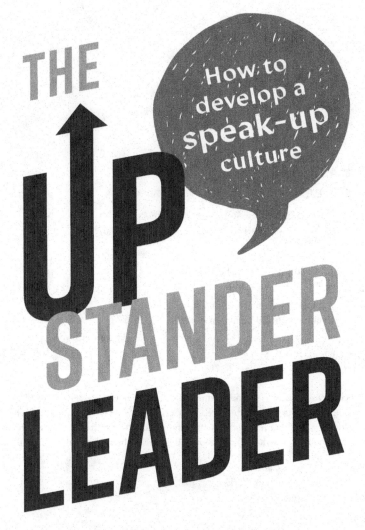

How to
develop a
speak-up
culture

UP
STANDER
LEADER

JESSICA HICKMAN

MAJOR
STREET

MAJOR STREET

First published in 2022 by Major Street Publishing Pty Ltd
info@majorstreet.com.au | +61 421 707 983 | majorstreet.com.au

© Jessica Hickman 2022
The moral rights of the author have been asserted.

A catalogue record for this book is available
from the National Library of Australia

Printed book ISBN: 978-1-922611-46-8
Ebook ISBN: 978-1-922611-47-5

Cover design by Tess McCabe
Internal design by Production Works
Author photo by Sophie Durham

10 9 8 7 6 5 4 3 2 1

Disclaimer

The material in this publication is in the nature of general comment only, and neither purports nor intends to be advice. Readers should not act on the basis of any matter in this publication without considering (and if appropriate taking) professional advice with due regard to their own particular circumstances. The author and publisher expressly disclaim all and any liability to any person, whether a purchaser of this publication or not, in respect of anything and the consequences of anything done or omitted to be done by any such person in reliance, whether whole or partial, upon the whole or any part of the contents of this publication.

Contents

Introduction: My breaking point   1

PART I: Bystanders   11

Chapter 1   The change era   13
Chapter 2   Why bystanders create toxic cultures   23

PART II: Upstanders   35

Chapter 3   The upstander effect   37
Chapter 4   The upstander generation   53
Chapter 5   The upstander and bystander zones   63
Chapter 6   The new age – empathy, ethics and equality   79

PART III: The Five Steps to Becoming an Upstander   93

Chapter 7   Look   95
Chapter 8   Listen   107
Chapter 9   Learn   125
Chapter 10   Lead   139
Chapter 11   Love   155

Conclusion   169
About the author   173
Acknowledgements   175
References   177

Introduction

My breaking point

In June 2017, I was lying in a hospital bed – fearful, burned out and hopeless. I had been admitted after collapsing at work with suspected appendicitis… but the cause was much less easy to remove.

For three and a half years I had been tormented by a bully in my workplace. I had started to develop severe anxiety. My body was in constant fight-flight-or-freeze mode. My bully would nudge my desk, yell at me, berate me in meetings and accuse me of having interpersonal relationships with clients. And so many people did nothing to stop it.

It breaks my heart – but it also makes me incredibly determined – to think back on my hospital admission and my long road to recovery. I was disappointed and hurt that I had given my life to build a culture in this workplace. I had won all these awards and been the public face of the company, yet behind the scenes they could not deal with the one bad apple that was ruining it for us.

I was so traumatised by the experience that I pretended I was going back to the UK, but I secretly moved to Sydney instead. Since then, I have dedicated my career to making sure nobody has to feel the way I felt at the hands of a workplace bully, or like a cog in a toxic workplace.

As the founder of Bullyology and driver of the Upstander movement, I've used my background in human resources, workplace health and safety, coaching and behavioural therapy to guide organisations and individuals on how to create healthier workplaces that are free from conflict.

By leaving Darwin and moving to Sydney, I was able to get a new perspective. I could look back, pause and reflect on the previous three and a half years – a tornado that had swept me up and spat me out.

In this space and time, I was able to think about my experience and about bullying, harassment and toxic cultures. I also thought about why good people – and most of all leaders – would stand by, watch and do nothing. This led me to found Bullyology and go on a journey to uncover some of the reasons why toxic behaviours are allowed to manifest unseen in organisations – and the statistics are alarming.

The way we work (at our worst)

Almost half of Australians will suffer some form of workplace bullying during their career. Safe Work Australia estimates that workplace bullying costs employers in Australia up to $36 billion per annum, and that the problem is getting worse, not better. Claims of mental stress, bullying and harassment have risen over the past two years. So, what's causing this? Is it the increasing demands of the workplace? Is it the change in working styles and arrangements due to COVID-19?

While leaders today, in organisations small and large, are overwhelmed with to-do lists that boggle their mind, a big problem is brewing. As a leader, you may be struggling to build a business, keep a division or team on track and deliver great products, results and services. Meanwhile, toxic behaviour in your workplace may be going unnoticed and unchecked.

Most leaders I work with are shocked to discover that bad behaviours, bullying and harassment are running out of control like a bushfire across their business or organisation. Not only are these behaviours present, they're having business ramifications because they are damaging employee wellbeing, top-line profits and business successes, as well as leader reputations and future opportunities.

Ironically, these behaviours add hours to leaders' schedules when left unchecked. They become the elephant in the room in workplaces and industries across Australia and beyond. Thankfully, it's getting harder and harder for bullies to hide, especially in high-profile organisations: from tech startups to government agencies, toxic workplaces are making headlines.

While writing this book, a prominent example came to light. A team from the Australian Broadcasting Corporation spoke to 100 current and former staff of Sony Music Australia, who shared allegations of the toxic culture of bullying and harassment at one of Australia's biggest record companies. Long-time CEO Denis Handlin allegedly dressed as Hitler (which was captured on video), threw tantrums over a meat pie, took trips to brothels and participated in bullying, sexual harassment and discrimination. The company was willing to turn a blind eye for decades. We're living in times when this behaviour can no longer be tolerated.

Knowing what you know now and reflecting on the behaviours you have seen or experienced in your career, what cost to your workplace productivity are you prepared to tolerate? Are you prepared to just stand by?

Today, toxic leaders who might have swept the issues under the carpet in the past are being called out in the newspapers and social media. You are a leader who is choosing to be proactive before events become reactive. And this book will help you to do just that.

The flow-on effect of a toxic culture

Bullying in the workplace affects not only the target – it also causes missed opportunities and lost profits. Leaders who are ill-equipped to deal with the bullying scourge permeating their culture and affecting morale and employee wellbeing are less efficient in the business's growth.

Let's take the bottom line, for example. The Australian Human Rights Commission noted the following consequences employers face when workers are bullied:

- higher absenteeism and turnover
- lower morale and decreased productivity
- legal and workers compensations
- time lost for managers dealing with the issues.

Bullying costs the Australian economy up to $36 billion per year, with the average case amounting to $17,000 to $24,000 for employers – and this is even if it doesn't escalate to a legal battle. Workplace stress alone costs the nation more than $14 billion annually. If I reflect on my own workplace bullying experience, I was sick a lot more. My body was run-down and fatigued. A Safe Work Australia report linked depression to increased absenteeism and low productivity, amounting to an $8 billion annual cost to the Australian economy. The same study found that mitigating bullying and strain could save 8.66 per cent of this financial burden.

Employees who have faced bullying in the workplace may experience a number of issues, including stress, depression, illness, insomnia and even suicidal thoughts. As the House Standing Committee on Education and Employment reported in 2012, this indicates that the consequences influence the worker's life outside the office as well, infiltrating all day-to-day activities, from family life to broader social engagement.

In my own bullying experience, everything was impacted. I was so unhappy at work that I would spend my time on the weekend either drinking copious amounts of wine to numb the pain of another week of hell, or burnt out in bed, unable to socialise or communicate.

Why should you read this book?

After my lengthy personal ordeal of workplace bullying, I found the courage to become an advocate for change. I educated myself in the fields of bullying and mental health in workplaces, schools and online environments. In my position, I became aware of the toxic cultures that permeated organisations and industries, and of the sheer lack of conversations around psychological safety, wellbeing and effective upstanding leadership, especially with regard to creating thriving workplace cultures.

I learned the core lessons and values that would later spark and inform my mission to be a change maker dedicated to creating safe and supportive work environments. My internationally recognised efforts in advocating for workplace safety, cultural change and proactive, future-focused leadership has led me to receive numerous ministerial and industry awards.

I believe that from adversity comes power, and I now help others understand the complex nature of modern bullying. I spend my days speaking, consulting and running workshops for C-suite executives, business owners, leaders and employees on how to create psychologically safe, thriving workplace cultures free from bullying, harassment and toxicity. My work centres on modernising mindsets, challenging unconscious biases and building upstanders who are future-ready leaders.

I am reinventing the way anti-bullying is taught, with a strong focus on cause and effect that prioritises employee productivity, psychological safety, health and wellbeing. My time-tested techniques and real-world strategies incorporate the latest in bullying and harassment research, giving every level of an organisation the knowledge, culture and confidence it needs to tackle a complex, health-harming global issue that can massively impact performance and success.

We are in an era in which outrage agendas, division and selfishness have been considered to be more productive for success than kindness, empathy and understanding. *The Upstander Leader* is timely. Toxicity is a game with no winners. The notion of teamwork gets derailed when voices of the loud and intimidating override the rest. Broken cultures and leadership seeking ultimate power lead businesses to self-destruct.

A workplace that actively promotes a positive culture and proactively handles bullying incidents is much better equipped to protect what matters the most – the staff and the business reputation. Failing to address bullying costs money, wastes time and alienates employees.

In this book, I share my personal story of workplace bullying and help you, as a leader, to understand how damaging bullying can be for your personal, company and team success. I share this story not for therapy nor for revenge, but for education and awareness. My intent is to mitigate risk and protect you as a leader.

I have a dream of seeing employee wellbeing and mental health being prioritised within companies, and education around such topics being provided to employees in an accessible and affordable manner. I have a vision that my work can encourage people to take ownership of their personal and mental wellbeing, which will in turn see a decline in the levels of workplace bullying. I want employees to feel empowered to be upstanders.

So, what is an upstander?

In my workshops, talks and digital resources, I focus on moving people 'from bystanders to upstanders'. So, what is that exactly?

The term 'upstander' has been around for a little while now. It refers to an individual or group that makes the conscious decision to stand up for their beliefs and values, and be proactive about positive change. An upstander recognises when something is wrong and acts to make it right.

The term has popped up in the vocabulary of human rights activists and organisations worldwide, including former United States Ambassador to the United Nations Samantha Power and the non-profit group Facing History and Ourselves.

In 2014, a petition was created by a school organisation to bring the word 'upstander' into the dictionary. They commented: 'This past year, the words "selfie," "twerk," and "badassery" made their way into the English dictionary. While these words have interwoven themselves into everyday speech, there is another far more important word that deserves proper recognition: **upstander**'.

Fast-forward to today, and thousands of people are now under-standing and embodying the term 'upstander' and taking action to help others in their workplaces, schools and communities.

Every leader can become a true upstander, whether by challenging negative stereotypes within their workplace, standing up to a toxic bully or championing cultural change. As a leader, you have the power to make choices that will shape history, your organisation's culture and your leadership legacy. You risk damage to your reputation if you don't pay attention to the big-picture trends affecting global and local workplaces.

We have seen an upswell of global change driven by upstanders – people who want to create social change. We are in the midst of the fourth industrial revolution and the digital revolution, and the future of work is shifting and changing. This book touches upon our innate desire as members of an evolutionary society to inspire change, positively disrupt the status quo and have our voices shared.

I created my company Bullyology and have written *The Upstander Leader* to promote lasting and necessary change in the workplace. I currently deliver programs that can be adapted to an organisation's specific needs, putting the employer in a position to be a change maker and upstander. I am seeking to ensure that the organisations I work with are optimally productive, safe, legally compliant, and free from bullying and harassment. It has been repeatedly shown that targeted education is the best way to counteract the high social, health and financial costs associated with toxic environments, whether online or in corporate or educational environments.

What's coming up?

I have structured *The Upstander Leader* around my five-step methodology. To introduce this, I unpack the upswell of global change being caused by upstanders and how it's impacting your workplace, and I explain the bystander effect in detail.

I want to help you understand that, as a leader, you hold the key to transforming your workplace culture. In my experience, people are promoted to leadership positions because they are good at their trade or an expert in their area, but they're often not given the essential information on big-picture trends that would enable them to understand their role and responsibility as a leader. You must understand the trends that are emerging and evolving in this decade of disruption to impact your workplace culture. Otherwise, you risk potential damage to your reputation, your leadership and your employees' growth and productivity.

In 2021, I moved from Sydney out to Orange in the Central West region of New South Wales. This was four years after I started Bullyology, and the movement was beginning to grow. At the time, I was conducting a range of workshops and lectures, and facilitating training sessions across multiple industries. They centred on psychological safety, future-focused leading and upstanding.

Through this, I worked with a local council. When I started working with the council, we were looking at both global and local trends that could impact their workplace culture. Throughout that process, the number-one factor I found was that leaders didn't have an adequate awareness of some of the big-picture trends that were happening on a global scale, such as emerging technologies; the rise in movements against injustice; bullying and harassment conversations; and other trends we will discuss in this book.

I have found this throughout many industries that I have worked with, both in regional towns and in cities across Australia and beyond. It's important to understand and conduct conversations about what it means to be an upstander and a future-focused leader.

As a leader, it's your responsibility to learn, grow and evolve – to be a model for your employees. I have found in my work that leaders who don't pay attention to these big-picture trends fall behind and alienate themselves or their employees through a lack of communication. This results in a toxic, outdated environment and culture that can cause psychological, emotional and physical damage to all parties. When working with leaders, I always tell them how important it is to maintain your reputation, because shit sticks. If you are allowing or participating in toxic behaviours, that ultimately can lead to reputation damage within your team and organisation, and externally.

In this book, I explore the times you might have become a bystander in your own life, and challenge your thinking, including your own unconscious biases. I introduce you to the upstander effect, and show how bullying, harassment and toxic behaviours are the problem and the upstanders are the solution. It's about reframing our language. This is not about whistleblowing; this is about building champions of workplace culture. Our focus is on the proactive rather than the reactive, and on understanding that empathy, ethics and equality are the bedrock for success.

I will never forget how I felt in that hospital bed. I was so depleted, so worn down and so broken. I never want anyone to feel that way, even to a lesser degree: to fear speaking up in a Zoom meeting, or feel their stomach drop when a certain colleague walks into the elevator with them.

We can all play a part in changing workplace culture and become upstanders, not bystanders. By the end of this book, I hope you will feel proud of your role in changing how colleagues and leaders can work together and uplift each other. Employees, leaders and consumers, the time for change is now!

BYSTANDERS

Our world is changing. Are you going to be a bystander, ignoring change as it happens around you? Or are you going to be an upstander, contributing to positive change?

Chapter 1

The change era

I was born and raised in Wales, where I found my passion for social justice. At the age of 14, I began volunteering and started a career working in youth and homeless shelters. I have always been drawn to social-impact work and helping others, especially vulnerable people and communities who might not have been served similar opportunities as others who were more fortunate. I was provided with mentoring and coaching to grow my leadership skills, until eventually I was running youth drop-in centres and became a community leader.

When I moved to Australia in 2013 and took a human resources position with a Darwin-based oil and gas project, I was confident I could continue to have a positive impact on the people I worked with. And I did, but it wasn't easy, as I had a new manager at my company decided to make my life a misery (more on that later)!

I've always had a desire to make a difference. It might be because of the millennial generation I was born into. Increasingly, young people are campaigning for change, whether it's fighting to protect the planet or personal freedoms.

On a global scale, change makers are rallying for action around the social causes of our time. Whether we're fighting for change in our communities or playing a part in combating global issues, we can make a difference.

Think about some of the trends that have grown at lightning speed and that you, your friends and your colleagues have discussed. What are some of the movements and ideas of recent times that stand out to you as needing our attention?

Is AI a kinder colleague than you?

The primary movement causing this revolution is the dominance of technology in business. How we work is shifting, evolving and changing, and this change has been accelerated by the recent COVID-19 pandemic and our subsequent reliance on technology to connect, learn and teach. However, as with all advancements – especially rapid ones – the rise of technology and all the personal and global information now at our fingertips can be both empowering and debilitating, with the power to free the modern worker or make them a slave to a machine.

Emerging technologies are having a profound effect on the way we interact with our fellow humans. Businesses that are not future-focused and thinking about the technology boom will be left behind in the next decade. Jobs are becoming more automated, which counterintuitively places a greater emphasis on human behaviour and the vital need for us to develop our interpersonal skills in areas such as empathy, ethics, equality, compassion and authentic leadership. The emergence of new technologies and artificial intelligence (AI) means that we're having to look at ourselves as humans and how we're showing up in comparison.

Technology and scientific advancements have made the world a better place. There have been improvements to our quality of life and work efficiency. We can work whenever, from wherever. Being able to communicate from wherever allows us to access more opportunities for cultural information, knowledge and resources. For someone like myself, being from the UK but based in Australia, I lean on technology as a means of connection to my family and also to do business on a global scale.

However, while working with leaders across industries, I have found that technology has sometimes become a barrier to success. With employees working from home, leaders have become micro-managers because they're unsure how to lead in this new world where technology is in between them and their employees. Gartner's research around data analysis shows that 16 per cent of employers are using technologies more frequently to monitor their employees, through methods such as virtual clocking in, tracking work computers and monitoring employee emails and internal communications.

Technology has also led to a lot of leaders and workers experiencing burnout, because there's no work-life balance when we're working from home and we've got our devices following us to bed. We check our emails in the middle of the night and again when we wake up in the morning. There's no off button.

There's also a privacy risk that comes with emerging and current technology. Advancements in social media open up the risk of reputation damage for leaders – they may have posted something on social media that has come back around to bite them, or a toxic email or conversation may have ended up in the media.

We are also seeing a rise in cyberbullying. Some people are happy to use technology to participate in toxic behaviour, to hide behind their keyboards and become 'keyboard warriors'. In 2021, I was a double finalist in the Orange Business Awards. I posted about it on LinkedIn and someone wrote a nasty, negative, toxic comment. I did not know this person, but he commented, 'They'll give awards to anyone these days'. One click of a button and I could see where he worked, who his employer was and what his job title was. I was able to look at the trail of his conversations and see that he was abusing a lot of people on LinkedIn.

I contacted his employer and sent them a screenshot of his comment. I also shared it on LinkedIn as a learning point, removing his name and asking my peer group how they would have responded. Someone I know contacted me and told me that this person had been abusing some of their employees. It is fortunate that I was able to nip it in the bud. I am hopeful that this cyberbully's employer subsequently had a conversation with him, and appropriate action was taken.

As a leader, how are you managing the technology within your teams? Are you having conversations about how damaging it can be? What are some of the behaviours you've witnessed online as a leader that you may have scrolled past and thought, 'They're not my problem'? Remember that this isn't about being a whistleblower; this is about being an upstander against toxic abuse.

Exercise: Look at your technology health

Are you switching off your devices and giving yourself that work-life balance, or are your phone and email following you to bed? How do you communicate with your team and staff? Do you pick up the phone and have conversations, or is it all one-sided directions via email? Is your technology your friend or enemy?

Sharing, spreading and storing information

We are in a data revolution, as well. Access to a wealth of data means we can absorb more news and information than at any other time in history. Knowledge is power, and it is at our fingertips. Being more aware of what's happening in the world makes us better at taking action and doing something about inequality and unfairness. Have you got your finger on the pulse with the data and information that's now accessible and available to you?

Data provides leaders with opportunities and fuel for better decision-making. It can increase productivity, reduce costs for organisations, and help companies improve customer service and build trust with employees, customers and brands. It can also lead to more innovation across industries. It can highlight the need for culture change, and it can help change corporate culture. It can be gathered to support the facts and get feedback, and to show how employees, leaders and people within organisations are feeling. Pulse checks have been important during the pandemic.

However, it's important to know how to use data for good. There is a definite bias in data collection: data experts are starting to unpack the under-representation of minorities with regards to data. There can also be poor-quality data, or a lack of data around a specific subject. Some trends are being supported by limited information.

It can be limiting to rely too much on data and forget to rely on the human element of connection and communication. A recent client of mine showed me a workplace culture survey in which they thought they had used data to their advantage. However, while unpacking this survey, we realised that it was very biased and asked closed questions that validated the assumptions of the person who conducted the survey. It's always important to get external advice when collecting a data set.

As a leader, it is important to question how you are using data. Something that I spend a lot of time doing in my business is supporting leaders in checking the pulse of their workplace culture. As management guru Peter Drucker said, what you don't measure, you can't manage. Are you measuring the things that matter and making sure you're looking after the humans within your business, not just the product or the top line?

When conducting a pulse check, it is helpful to break questions into four categories:

1. Organisational culture:
   - Would you recommend your organisation as a great place to work?
   - What words and phrases would you use to describe the current culture – 'the way we do things around here'?
   - What words or phrases would you use to describe the type of culture you need?

2. People and teams:
   - Describe the relationships within your team.
   - Describe your sense of belonging in the team.
   - How have you witnessed bullying or harassment in the workplace?
   - How proactive are leadership in dealing with bullying and harassment?
   - How emotionally well do you feel at work?

3. Your role:
   - What feedback is provided to you regarding your performance and growth?
   - How involved are you in decisions that affect your work?
   - How do you get rewarded for your efforts?
   - How could learning and development be improved?

4. The future:
   - How can your organisation modernise the way it works?
   - If you were the CEO and you had a magic wand, what would be the first action you would take to work on culture?
   - What is the desirable future for you at your organisation?

Globalisation and diversity

We are living in a more connected world than ever before. Our world is more diverse, exposing us to new cultures and ideas we may have not experienced before. Our ability to challenge the status quo increases when we're exposed to a wider range of innovative ideas, cultural concepts and challenging viewpoints.

The COVID-19 pandemic has ushered us into the new way and world of working. It is now easier than ever to work with people from across the globe. In my previous workplace, when I was working on an oil and gas project, we had people of 52 different nationalities working on the project. My support partners in my current business are in the Philippines and are skilled at doing all things web and back-end; thanks to globalisation, I've had the opportunity to partner with them.

Our new globalised world necessitates conversations, strategies and change around diversity, inclusion and belonging to ensure that we are incorporating and nurturing human rights. Diversity and inclusion provide opportunities to become more open, to learn, to be flexible and to appreciate cultural differences.

Like anything, globalisation and diversity come with some major risks. The one I want to focus on is something you may have seen in your workplace culture: I've seen a lot of discrimination happening. There can be a loss of culture and traditions, and there can be bias in the recruiting process. Diversity and inclusion need attention. We're seeing a lot of companies invest in this as a function, but I'd like you to unpack how you can personally harness this in your own workplace. We're going to look at discrimination, empathy, ethics and equality as we move through the book.

Authors Liz Fosslien and Mollie West Duffy explain: 'Diversity is having a seat at the table, inclusion is having a voice, and belonging is having that voice be heard'. Creating an environment in which employees understand what it means to be inclusive earns them a sense of belonging.

When we think about discrimination, diversity and globalisation, one of the recent movements that we need to pay attention to is the Black Lives Matter (BLM) movement. This highlighted the systemic racism that is happening on a global scale and made me aware of some of the systemic racism in Australia, which affects some of the clients I've been working with. This then led me to unpack some of my own unconscious biases.

My good friend Natalie Welch shared in one of our collaboration workshops that one of her leadership clients had identified around 20 of their own unconscious biases. Following the BLM movement, I went on a mission to read 15 to 20 books and talk to a diverse range of people to understand systemic racism and learn as much as possible about the BLM movement.

If you're not already doing so, chat to some of your peers and employees from different cultural backgrounds to get an idea of how they're feeling about up-and-coming movements for change. How do they feel that your organisation or you as a leader are harnessing their voice and providing space for diverse opinions?

Actively learn in this space and see how you can evolve your thought patterns around creating an equal and equitable work environment for all.

The ideas revolution

As a leader, you must understand that we're also in the midst of an ideas revolution, in which new concepts are experiencing exponential growth. New ideas are spreading like wildfire. We're in the era of ideas going viral within half a second. We are seeing the emergence of the ability to craft a message and amplify it at lightning speed.

Many grassroots movements are rising. These are the ideas and social causes that have been established around kitchen tables and developed into global discussions – causes such as eliminating racism, enabling sexual liberation and female anatomical rights, and taking action on climate change. The ideas revolution aligning with the fourth industrial revolution means that leaders and people like ourselves can partner with people across the globe to collaborate, innovate and create groundbreaking ideas and research.

This also means, however, that bad behaviours can be outed and spread at the speed of light. If you participate in bad workplace behaviours or don't deal with bad workplace behaviours, you can become a household name in the media. This can cause reputation damage, which can create negative perceptions about your company and about you as a leader.

Fiction can also spread like wildfire. In recent times, we've seen many different rumours and accusations being circulated on social media. For example, celebrity deaths: anyone on a social media network has seen the rumours, or as Donald Trump would frequently say, 'fake news'. Justin Bieber has been one of the most common celebrity death hoax victims in the history of the internet.

The good news is that positive ideas can spread just as quickly as bad ideas. The pandemic has been a catalyst for a positive ideas revolution – throughout the pandemic we've seen TikTok dances and challenges going viral, building momentum and creating change. Another example occurred in the summer of 2014, when millions of people around the world took the ALS Ice Bucket Challenge to spread awareness and raise money for amyotrophic lateral sclerosis (ALS) research. The challenge raised an estimated $135 million worldwide, with $4 million of that going to the ALS Therapy Development Institute.

Another powerful movement that has emerged is the #MeToo movement. This highlighted an epidemic of sexual harassment in the workplace, gaining momentum across the world and exposing the outrageous behaviours that often get swept under the carpet. Following on from this in Australia was the March4Justice, organised in response to the alleged rape of political staffer Brittany Higgins, which highlighted a large-scale culture of silence and leaders not taking appropriate action. Movements like this can be a risk to you as a leader if you are walking by these behaviours or tolerating them within your organisation.

What have I learned?

In this chapter, we've unpacked some of the big-picture trends that are impacting you now and will impact your future as a leader. We must unite for change. We've seen that one voice can change the world. As a leader, are you using your voice to be that beacon of light?

We are in a decade of change and disruption that has been accelerated by the COVID-19 pandemic. We are in uncertain times, navigating uncharted waters as the world changes and we face unprecedented challenges.

As the status quo is being challenged, you need to be proactive rather than reactive. Explore your own leadership. Look at your own workplace culture and think about whether you are allowing any toxic mindsets or behaviours. Be aware of how technology – and the information it offers – can help you to create a culture of either freedom or fear. How can you learn more to get ahead of change?

Be curious about your own leadership, your people and your workplace culture. Lean into this topic. Explore and examine how you can be future-ready right now.

Chapter 2

Why bystanders create toxic cultures

The bystander effect is the enemy of a positive and thriving workplace culture. Bystanders allow toxic culture to be dismissed, worsening the problem. In this chapter, you'll conduct a self-inquiry about situations in which you've become a passive bystander and unpack your own unconscious biases. You will reflect on your own workplace's culture and the behaviours that you have witnessed, tolerated and accepted as a leader.

It is vital for you, as a leader, to understand the bystander effect as a disease. If left unchecked, toxic culture festers, spreads and leads to serious harm for employees, leaders and business success. Understanding the bystander effect will aid you to become a more conscious leader. It will help you nip problems in the bud. A strong and proactive consciousness of your environment will help you recognise the extent and impact of toxic workplace cultures, and will help you build an upstander culture, which is something we will explore in later chapters.

I know firsthand how the bystander effect can contribute to the manifestation of a toxic culture. My story outlines some serious leadership failures that were caused by bystanders who chose to accept, tolerate and walk by sustained workplace abuse, bullying and harassment.

I want you to understand by reading my story that everyone, unfortunately, is at risk of being bullied and of becoming a bully in their leadership position. This risk, and the mitigation of it in your position, is what I will be helping you unpack – because even the most clued-in person can find themselves acting as a bystander without even realising it.

The bystanders to my bullying

When I joined a company in Darwin, it was unfamiliar territory to me, but I learned a lot – very quickly. In the UK, I had spent time working in construction, oil and gas as an office manager for a large scaffolding company. Having the opportunity to work for a scaffolding company on a large project in Australia was same same, but different.

One of the different things that I established early on was that there was a fly-in fly-out (FIFO) culture in Australia. Men and women were living in camps for a month or more. They were away from friends and family, and would travel four hours or more on a flight interstate back to their loved ones.

After hearing the mental health stats around the FIFO industry and how high the suicide rate was, I made a commitment to use my skills and knowledge to create a thriving culture and make sure every employee who came through our HR department felt seen, nurtured and trusted.

However, my active role in supporting the workforce didn't protect me from parts of the toxic culture.

When a new HR manager joined the project, my life changed. I was responsible for his training and showing him the systems and the ropes. At first, he was quiet and sat back, but when he got promoted into a leadership position, things drastically changed. I vividly recall, on the first day of his promotion, him threatening that if I didn't like the way he wanted things done or the fact that he was now the leader, he would bring in his own people. He also reminded me that I was on a company-sponsored work visa – looking back, I realised this was a subtle threat that I could potentially be deported from the country if I didn't do what he said, because the company technically owned my visa.

After that, a pattern of sustained bullying and harassment grew over a period of three and a half years. Being young, naive and very early on in my career, I didn't notice some of the signs. He began making sexist comments, such as, 'Women are only good for one thing'. He insulted my appearance. He undermined my work. He assigned me unrealistic work tasks and then berated me publicly when I was inevitably unable to complete them, accusing me of incompetence. Meanwhile, I was winning a slew of national and local awards, including being nominated for Exceptional Young Woman in Resources and Northern Territory Young Achiever of the Year.

I reported this bullying and harassment 32 times, and 32 times I was met with false promises and assurances that it would be dealt with. I had side chats, tears, heartache, sleepless nights, vomiting and a post-traumatic stress disorder (PTSD) diagnosis, and still the bullying continued.

This is the bystander effect in the worst-case scenario: seeing a woman sitting in front of you begging for help and not making the uncomfortable decision to help her because there'll be too much paperwork, the conversation will be too hard, or you just don't want to deal with what's happening.

Exercise: Does my story trigger a memory?

Pause and reflect on my story. What feelings come up for you? If you had been a leader in this organisation and you had seen or heard about the bullying, what questions would you have asked me? What measures or steps would you have taken as a leader? What conversations would have needed to be had? What would have happened with the bully, and how or where would you have documented this? Does anything else come to mind that hasn't been considered?

Unpacking the bystander effect

As a leader, it's important to understand the bystander effect, and how good people can stand by and allow negative behaviours to create and breed toxic culture. The bystander effect occurs when the presence of others discourages an individual (or several individuals) from intervening in an emergency situation against a bully, or during an assault or crime.

The greater the number of bystanders, the less likely it is for any one of them to help the person in distress. People are more likely to take action in a crisis when there are fewer witnesses present.

Let me give you an example. You're driving down the highway and see a car on the side of the road that has had an accident. There seem to be witnesses attending to the car. You drive past, automatically thinking, 'They'll be all right' (or the Aussie standard, 'She'll be right, mate').

Reflecting on this and my own workplace bullying experience led me to think about how many people witnessed, walked by and tolerated the bullying I experienced – the verbal abuse, the folders being thrown across the room.

It made me realise that, at times, there were 10 to 13 people that could have witnessed the bullying in that open-plan office. It also led me to think about deferred responsibility in managers' meetings, where there would be seven or eight men around the table when toxic comments were directed at me.

My colleagues would roll their eyes or come and quietly chat to me afterwards. However, on reflection, they always looked to the highest-paid person in the room – the project manager, the leader or the CEO – to deal with the behaviour. The attitude was, 'Not my problem, not my issue'.

The term 'bystander effect' was coined by social psychologists Bibb Latané and John Darley. They popularised the concept following the 1964 murder of a young lady called Kitty Genovese in New York City. Kitty was a 28-year-old woman who was brutally stabbed to death outside her apartment while on her way home from work. At the time, it was reported that there were dozens of neighbours who failed to step in and assist her or call the police. Some reports even mentioned up to 38 witnesses who had observed, heard or walked by the scene.

When the police investigated, it was found that no one had called the police at the time. There was a deferring of responsibility or social influence. Latané and Darley attributed the bystander effect to two factors:

1. The more onlookers there are, the less personal responsibility an individual feels to take action.
2. Individuals monitor the behaviours of others around them to determine how to act.

This is important for us to understand because it is present in our day-to-day behaviours.

Exercise: Your closest bystanders

As a leader, think about why some bystanders don't intervene in your workplace. Reflect on the times in your career when you have been a bystander and not spoken up, intervened in or challenged toxic behaviours. Here are some of the reasons I have heard from leaders at my workshops:

- 'We did not know what to do or how to report it, because we had a lack of training.'
- 'We were unsure about what constitutes unacceptable behaviour, or whether it was bullying or harassment.'
- 'We feared speaking up may lead to the bully turning on us, or the bully's cronies or upper management targeting us.'
- 'We didn't feel that we had the numbers on our side.'
- 'We had inadequate peer support.'
- 'I thought it was none of my business because it wasn't affecting me and my team.'
- 'I wasn't confident that management would support me if I spoke up.'
- 'I thought that speaking up would make things worse.'
- 'I didn't want to draw attention to myself.'
- 'I felt that the victim may deserve it, because they had a personal agenda against the bully.'
- 'I was worried that the workplace's "my way or the highway" leadership style could effectively make me lose my job for speaking up.'

Whatever the reason for not speaking up, I have found in my work and research that the consequences of doing nothing are worse. The unacceptable behaviour doesn't change and may spiral out of control. A lack of intervention from peers can give the bullies the green light to continue the toxic behaviour. Being a bystander and silently watching can also lead you to become an actively harmful perpetrator: because you choose not to intervene, the perpetrator may pressure you into participating in the bullying, harassment or toxic behaviour. People may also feel increased anxiety about the failure to report the incident, which could ultimately cause more harm.

There are many factors we need to understand about why some people become bystanders. Sometimes we just don't have the skills, knowledge, tools or understanding to know how to be an upstander rather than a bystander.

The cold, hard truth is that one bad apple can spoil a whole bunch. Just take my workplace bullying experience, for example. The bully caused the other employees to operate in a state of fear, discomfort and avoidance. I work with teams and organisations across Australia and beyond, and I find that sometimes the workplace culture is ruined by one toxic person, who then recruits cronies to help them with their campaign of belittlement.

Bystanders aren't all bad people

The bystander effect is not limited just to bullying, harassment and toxic behaviours. As we move through this chapter, conduct some self-inquiry about situations in which you were a passive bystander – not because you're a bad person, but because you simply didn't see, you were socially conditioned into thinking the situation was normal, or because of your own unconscious biases.

It's important as a leader to identify these situations, because being in tune with what's happening in your environment can help potentially save a life, make you a better leader and help you challenge the status quo. By questioning your unconscious biases and bystander behaviours, you can become an upstander leader.

There are many injustices that exist within the workplace and our communities. These injustices include abuse and neglect, racism, gender inequality, bullying, sexual harassment, the stigma around mental health, and even the emphasis on power and authority over kindness.

When my mother visited me a few years back in Darwin, we were in a taxi heading out to dinner and there was a lady asleep on the side of the road. My mother became visibly distressed and wanted to turn back to check if the lady was okay. I shrugged it off and said there were a lot of people on the streets homeless, drunk or begging for money in the Northern Territory. 'That person will be fine. It was normal behaviour.' My mother challenged me on this, which made me face my own unconscious bias and social conditioning. It reminded me of how distressed I had been when I first moved to Darwin and saw a lot of people on the streets either homeless or intoxicated. It was confronting and a bit of a culture shock.

In my early career, I worked for homeless projects, for the local council and in youth drop-in centres. Social impact, homelessness, addiction and supporting the community are things I am passionate about. Did this incident make me a bad person, or did I simply not see? Had I just been so socially conditioned to the behaviour that I assumed the person would be fine?

You'll be glad to know that we did pull over and check on the lady (who was intoxicated, and who swore at us and sent us packing), but it made me stop and look at my own behaviour. I'd been so caught up in my own internal world that I failed to scan my environment for things that could be a risk, and I forgot something I was passionate about.

This made me reflect on my own workplace and some of the bullying behaviours that became the social norm. Over time, people began to ignore the aggressive language and the flying folders. They made no eye contact as I was publicly berated. These behaviours came to be seen as normal.

As leaders, we can often fall into the trap of the bystander effect unknowingly, simply because we are busy and fail to observe some of the dynamics happening around us. Think about your workplace and your local community, and some of the interpersonal relationships that you have. What are some things you potentially haven't been noticing that could be improved if you paid attention to them?

Bystander archetypes

Like bullies and their targets, bystanders are not all the same. There are many characteristics and traits that influence how they respond (or don't respond) when someone else is in trouble, and that limit them from speaking up and standing up. Through speaking and delivering countless workshops for my business, Bullyology, I have been able to identify nine different archetypes of the bystander:

1. **The Oblivious:** These bystanders are either so socially unaware or unobservant that they fail to notice what's going on in front of their noses (unintentionally oblivious), or they have some level of awareness but choose to give the impression that they know nothing about the abuse (intentionally oblivious).

2. **The Anxious:** Choosing to step in and help someone can occasionally have negative consequences for the helper. They may fear losing their job, drawing the bully's attention towards them or making a difficult situation worse in some way. These fears can be perfectly valid or completely imagined; either way, the resulting anxiety discourages the bystander from taking action.

3. **The Naive:** This positive-thinking optimist assumes that the toxic behaviour will magically stop by itself at some point. Unfortunately, the rose-coloured 'wait and see' approach ignores

the historical reality that most bullying continues (and often gets worse) until decisive steps are taken to address it.

4. **The Unknowing:** Sometimes good people become silent bystanders simply because they're not sure what to do. Managers and employees in a workplace may not have the skills, tools, knowledge or training to know exactly how to intervene when a bullying incident occurs. This may be because the 'big bosses' don't see anti-bullying awareness, discussion or training as a priority. Unfortunately, in this case, ignorance is not bliss.

5. **The Uncaring:** 'It's not my problem' is this bystander's permanent mantra. They feel no social responsibility to do the right thing when something's wrong and take the 'better them than me' approach to any conflict. Empathy is nowhere to be seen in this 'everyone for themselves' philosophy.

6. **The Lazy:** These witnesses convince themselves there's no urgent need to help a person in strife because 'someone else will do it'. They may even have some minimal sympathy for the target but can't quite work up the motivation to do anything about it. Psychologists call this type of apathy 'altruistic inertia'.

7. **The Defeated:** Sometimes a bystander can feel so powerless that the idea of helping someone in need feels like a complete waste of time. They decide to give up before they try, convinced that nothing they do will make the slightest difference to the situation. Poor leadership in chronically noxious work cultures can create bystanders who feel incapable of being change makers.

8. **The Crony:** Not all bystanders are innocent. Some may be on the side of the bully (for whatever reason) and be either active or behind-the-scenes co-perpetrators. Even those who don't participate directly in the harassment may encourage it in

some way. Bullies love to have weak-willed lackeys around who condone or reinforce their aggressive actions.

9. **The Converger:** Remember back in your school days when there would be a fight in the schoolyard? Some kids would be keen to break it up, while others seemed to love the drama and would gravitate to the scene like bees to honey. These are the sight-seeing Convergers. They're easy to spot, loudly encouraging the conflict, enthusiastically filming the action or gossiping about it, with no concern that someone might get hurt. Many internet trolls are habitual Convergers.

Exercise: Own your part

Which of these archetypes most resonated with you, based on your current or past workplace experiences? Is there anything missing? If you could add a tenth archetype, what would it be?

Take courage in identifying your own bystander behaviours. Not all bystanders are bad people, so please be kind to yourself. Be curious and driven to learn more about how you can be an upstander leader – creating change and innovation, and supporting yourself, your team and your workplace culture.

At this stage, it's okay to feel a little bit flat. We've covered some big topics to elevate your awareness. From this point on, we'll be action oriented.

UPSTANDERS

So far, we've explored the problem. Let's switch gears and unpack the solution.

Chapter 3

The upstander effect

When I first joined the company in Darwin and learned about the frequent mental health struggles of employees, I put my hand up to be the Culture Lead and spend time helping to nurture the wellbeing of the staff. This was something I was passionate about even before my own bullying experience.

The culture program went from strength to strength, but it didn't happen overnight. As you can imagine, given I was a young Welsh woman standing in front of Kiwi and Aussie scaffolders saying, 'Let's talk about mental health', it came with building trust over time.

Something I committed to early on was to walk roughly six kilometres around the oil and gas project, day in and day out, building trust and respect within the workforce. I chatted to workers about their hobbies, their families and some of the reasons why they came to work away from home. The common thing I learned is they came for money but also to enhance quality of life outside of work for their family. I committed to making it my responsibility that everyone felt they had someone to talk to and trust, and that they could speak up if they were experiencing any mental health problems, isolation or loneliness.

We had a variety of issues that manifested due to people living away from home in the FIFO industry, such as addiction to gambling, drugs, alcohol and even sex. The experience gave me a deep, holistic view of some of the challenges facing people living in Australia, and specifically in construction and the FIFO industry.

I absolutely loved my role and the project. I loved my colleagues. We had created a community, a home away from home. Some of the office staff were from overseas or interstate, so company and culture was good – because we didn't have families to go home to, we had developed a 'work family' and often socialised outside of work. We were doing staff social events and I was in charge of it all. Being a social butterfly, I loved this responsibility.

It gave me a real taste of being an 'upstander' – a term I explored when I went on to start Bullyology. The 'upstander effect' is a term I created to challenge the acceptance of the bystander effect and create awareness around how being an upstander can and will change the world. In this chapter I'm going to talk about how you can join the movement.

Bullying, harassment and toxic behaviours are the root of the issue – and upstanders are there to find and become the solution. What effect do upstanders have on themselves and their environment? In this chapter, we're going to look deeply into and understand the upstander effect. We looked at what bystanders do and their effect in the previous chapter, so now let's look at the other side of the coin.

Many leaders are unaware of the effect they have on others. Let's not be those leaders. Let's be upstanding leaders who understand their power and influence. It can make or break your workplace culture.

Upstander culture makes your leadership easier. Fostering an environment of upstanders instead of bystanders can create a ripple effect and a strong leadership legacy. Why stand by when you can stand up?

Adam Goodes is one example of a true upstander. He is an Adnyamathanha man (an Aboriginal Australian), a former Australian Football League (AFL) player and a community leader who won Australian of the Year in 2014. He took a strong stand against racism, which led to him being racially abused at AFL matches on a regular basis.

In May 2013, for the first match of the Indigenous Round, his Sydney Swans were playing the Collingwood Magpies. Near the end of the game, with the Swans ahead, a 13-year-old girl and Collingwood supporter yelled at Goodes, calling him an ape. Goodes summoned security officers who ejected the girl from the grounds. Collingwood officials apologised to Goodes after the game.

The AFL supported him, but conservative commentator Andrew Bolt attacked Goodes for taking 'outsized offence at the rudeness of a girl'. Goodes was regularly booed at games from then on. The girl rang Goodes to apologise. Goodes commented publicly that, while it was not the first time he had been called 'monkey' or 'ape', it was shattering. He did not blame the girl herself. He said, 'I felt I was in high school again, being bullied, being called all these names because of my appearance. I didn't stand up for myself in high school, [but] I'm a lot more confident, I'm a lot more proud about who I am and my culture, and I decided to stand up last night and I'll continue to stand up'.

In June 2019, the AFL and its 18 clubs apologised to Goodes for failing to support him adequately in the face of this abuse. Since then, Adam has continued his quest to be a true upstander, raising awareness about racism and establishing the GO Foundation, which provides scholarships to Indigenous children from kindergarten through to university. Goodes is also an author of a children's book titled *Somebody's Land*, which raises awareness about racism and supports his culture and heritage.

The upstander effect, as shown by Goodes through his work, can help us fully appreciate the power of words to hurt people.

Adam Goodes showed courage and strength, and is a voice for other Indigenous people and sports stars.

Introducing the upstander effect

Becoming an upstander begins with awareness of our natural pull towards the bystander effect. It reaches fruition when we intentionally shift from being passive observers to proactive change makers.

By calling out injustice and abuse, we become purpose-driven initiators of positive culture. Positive effects of standing up include:

- empowering others to speak their truth
- encouraging policy and legislation change
- helping others understand their behaviours and unconscious biases
- giving a voice to those who have been silenced and can't yet speak up for themselves
- helping people who are paralysed by fear gain strength again
- shining a light on the elephant in many rooms
- initiating a butterfly effect, whereby small actions and changes can lead to big shifts
- increasing your own confidence, self-esteem and energy
- building important skills and capabilities
- improving relationships with others – either by fixing negative relationships or deepening pre-existing positive relationships
- improving overall quality of life, happiness and wellbeing
- helping people find the light at the end of a dark tunnel.

That being said, upstanders are often shocked to encounter backlash. When I stood up to my workplace bully, the backlash included an extreme physical threat from my bully. He stood over me with clenched fists and shouted in my face. My project leader turned against me, fearful that his incompetence was now in the open. He breached confidentiality by briefing witnesses with his version of the story, and lied during investigation about witnessing what had happened to cover his own back.

Colleagues withdrew and stopped engaging with me after being directed to by the bully. People avoided conversations about issues such as how toxic the culture really was. Well-meaning peers advised me to just ignore it and get on with it, but when I tried to do that, it made me more anxious, stressed and ill. My family became sick with fear about the impacts of the bullying and the lack of support following it.

While this seems confronting, doing the right thing always trumped standing by for me. Being bullied, and discovering how widespread the bullying was in my workplace and beyond, led me to recover my sense of self and my health. I learned to lean in and become a full-time upstander, which led to me developing my business Bullyology and driving the Upstander movement.

It's important to know what you're buying into as a leader when becoming an upstander. You need to be fully aware of all the impacts and effects that it can have. You'll have a positive impact, but there will potentially be backlash from friends, colleagues, peers or even family. Become an upstander with a holistic view of the pros and cons. This book will give you the awareness and capability to deal with the naysayers.

The upstanding people are all around us

Back in chapter 2, we unpacked the story of the bystander effect. I gave you an example of people driving by a car involved in an accident without stopping to help. I have a real-life example of this, of when I had a car accident and nearly died.

A couple of weeks before I left for Australia, I had a serious car accident in which my car got written off. Looking back now, I strongly believe that that experience also shaped and shifted the course of my life. The payout from the car ultimately set me up to stay in Australia and build a life. It also left me with a lasting lesson, as true upstanders intervened and saved me and my friends.

Four of my best friends had decided on a big day and night out watching rugby. In my eagerness to please and fear of missing out, I'd helpfully agreed to make a 45-minute journey to collect them at midnight. In Wales, when a rugby match is on, taxi prices are downright crazy. The girls had begged me to pick them up in exchange for a lower fare. Since I was saving for my trip to Australia in a few weeks, I figured I could certainly use the extra cash.

As I left, my mother asked me to please be careful. As any mother would be, she was worried about her 22-year-old daughter driving all that way at night alone. Looking fearful, she joked about packing a blanket and a toolkit. I hadn't been feeling well all day and anxiously got in the car. Along the way, I received several calls from my mates asking me to hurry up because my best friend was rather drunk. I wondered how interesting that would make the drive back. When I finally pulled up to the venue, the shoeless, tipsy girls all piled in the car, gossiping about the night's events, and we started to head back home.

All went smoothly until my best friend Tiffany announced that she was feeling sick. I pulled over, put her in the front seat and rolled down her window in case she needed to stick her head out and vomit along the way – not too elegant, but effective. As it turned out, this open window would play a critical role in our survival later.

I was driving cautiously in the slow lane when my back tyre blew. The car careered across the central strip and crossed two lanes. I realised I was losing complete control of my vehicle, and I was not sure what to do.

Desperately wrenching at the wheel and pulling hard on the hand brake, I tried to slow us down. I watched in what felt like slow motion as the car rolled down an embankment at high speed, bumping and rolling, tossing and turning. My whole life flashed before my eyes – it sounds clichéd, but it really does happen.

I must have briefly lost consciousness, because when I came to, my friend Holly was sprawled across my lap and unresponsive. Our car had crashed and landed on its side. I was now sideways, with my door unable to open since I was pressed against the ground. Tiffany dangled above me, suspended by her seatbelt.

An overwhelming feeling of panic surged through me. I don't know if it was because I could smell hot oil and was totally convinced the car could catch on fire, or because I was seriously overwhelmed with claustrophobia; either way, my survival instincts kicked in, and I remember thinking, 'Holy shit, I need to move quickly'.

Hannah, who was in the back seat, was sober enough to call emergency services, but we only had a vague idea of our location. Still dizzy, I mustered the strength to pull myself into an upright position and squeeze past the dangling Tiffany and out of the car through her open window, which now faced the sky. I tried to pull Tiffany through after me. It wasn't working. I thought, 'I've got to get out of this car and up to the highway to get some help'.

It was about 1 a.m. when I fought my way up a steep embankment through a mass of stinging nettles in a desperate bid to save my beloved best friends. I'd lost my footwear in the leap off the side of the car. As I frantically waited at the side of the road, a few cars screeched past me without slowing. One honked his horn loudly as he sped away. Dressed in my pyjamas with no shoes, hair covered in nettles and bleeding from a cut, I must have looked crazy – running in and out of the lanes trying to get a single car to stop.

The cars just drove by. Increasingly frustrated, I made the risky decision to run onto the highway to flag down a car.

As a car drove past, I threw myself into the lane, waving my hands. It swerved into the second lane to avoid me, and I thought it was gone. Then, about half a kilometre away, I could see the tail-lights begin to slow. I ran towards it like Usain Bolt, the soles of my bare feet collecting stray bits of motorway glass as I went.

The car had finally stopped, and the petrified older couple inside stared at me like stunned rabbits. I was crying, banging on the window and screaming for them to help me. Inside were my upstanders – the kind hearts who would save us.

I'll never forget the image of my four dear friends, still drunk and clearly shaking, huddled on top of the crushed car. After fighting their way through the stinging nettles, police and fire officers gently lifted each of the girls down and guided or carried them up the embankment. We were an unsightly mess, but we had survived.

The whole situation felt surreal. I was questioned by the police and asked to take a breath test, which of course came back completely negative.

I can distinctly recall the kindness I was shown in that vulnerable, traumatic time. The officer put a jacket around me, assured me I was safe and told me it wasn't my fault. Something on the road had exploded and torn my tyre into a million pieces.

Adrenaline only keeps you going for so long; then the body shuts down to protect itself. At that moment, I went into shock. It felt like time was standing still. I was strapped to a stretcher bed with my head and neck secured, on my side in a recovery position. I was shaking so badly that my head kept bouncing off the board, dangling sideways lifelessly. Staring out the back of the ambulance, I spied my drunk and mud-covered friends howling, crying and making blubbering phone calls, while three years' worth of my university paperwork was scattered across the highway.

A female police officer stood above me with tears rolling down her face. Her colleague comforted her. She said, 'When we got the call tonight that five girls were in a crushed vehicle that had rolled three times coming off the highway, I prepared for the worst – massive injuries or multiple fatalities. But you've all walked away from this with nothing but scratches and bruises. It's a miracle. Somebody is definitely looking after you'. When we hear about horrific car accidents, domestic violence that ends in tragedy, or grossly neglected children, we often forget about the first responders who have to deal with this kind of trauma on a regular basis and the emotional toll it takes on them.

Reflecting back to that incredibly frightening night, I can't even remember the faces of the people who helped me, but I can still feel their warmth, their empathy, their kindness and their support. These people were upstanders. They stood tall. They looked adversity in the face, and they came through it to make a difference when it really mattered. They were a positive force for good. They reminded me that it's not what you look like that defines you, or what you say, but how you make others around you feel.

The couple who stopped and helped me chose to overcome the bystander effect. They may have saved my life and my friends' lives. Their kindness made me appreciate life in a new way. Although I'll never know who they were, I felt their care, connection and kindness in a way that stays with me to this day. I am also deeply grateful for the emergency response officers who removed us safely from the car that was leaking oil.

Exercise: The positive effect of upstanders

Think about a time in your life when an upstander has had a positive effect on you. It might not be as drastic as my story. Perhaps someone has had your back or championed your success. When have you been an upstander?

The effect of upstanders past and present

Upstanders aren't a new idea. If we take time to reflect on other upstanders, we can recognise the effect they had and build it into our own leadership. Every leader I have worked with wants to leave a legacy and have their work remembered with respect; being more aware of your effect can help you do that.

Let's have a look at some notable examples of upstanders from the past and present, and the effect their upstanding has had on individuals, workplaces and society as a whole:

- **Nelson Mandela** (1918–2013) was an anti-apartheid leader. He spent over 20 years in jail for his opposition to the racist system that excluded black people from many areas of South African society. He was elected the first President of South Africa in 1994. He famously said, 'I have cherished the ideal of a democratic and free society in which all persons live together in harmony and with equal opportunities'. He showed that one person can have a big impact and circumstances don't determine the outcome (Mandela achieved his impact from a prison cell), highlighted the systemic nature of racism, and inspired so many people through his steely determination.

- **Ruth Bader Ginsburg** (1933–2020) was an associate justice of the Supreme Court of the United States and a staunch advocate for women's rights. An expert in international law, she rose to a powerful position of influence while defying sexual discrimination throughout her esteemed career. She showed that women must have a seat at the table, proved you can change the system from within, and served as a role model for women seeking gender equity and civil rights.

- **Martin Luther King** (1929–1968) was a non-violent civil rights leader. He inspired the American civil rights movement to achieve greater equality and helped organise the 1963 March on Washington for Jobs and Freedom, where he gave his famous 'I have a dream' speech. As he said in that iconic speech, 'I have a dream that one day this nation will rise up and live out the true meaning of its creed. We hold these truths to be self-evident: that all men are created equal'. He became a visionary who wasn't afraid to have big dreams, inspired and empowered others to have big dreams and aspirations, and gained respect and trust through speaking his truth.

- **Malala Yousafzai** (born 1997) is a Pakistani woman who, as a schoolgirl, defied Taliban threats and campaigned for her right to education. She survived being shot in the head by the Taliban and became a global advocate for women's rights – especially the right to education. She proved you're never too young to be an upstander, reminded women around the world that education is a basic human right, embodied a love of learning and a learning culture, and never gave up on her upstander quest even after being shot by the Taliban.

- **Abraham Lincoln** (1809–1865) was the President of the United States of America during the American Civil War. Lincoln issued the famous Emancipation Proclamation of 1863, declaring 'that all persons held as slaves' within the rebellious states 'are, and henceforward shall be free'. This proclamation was followed by the Thirteenth Amendment to the US Constitution in 1865, outlawing slavery. He challenged biases that were widespread and socially accepted, had a vision for change and communicated it with strength and purpose, and rallied support and enrolled others for change.

- **Mother Teresa** (1910–1997) was an Albanian nun and charity worker. Devoting her life to the service of the poor and dispossessed, Mother Teresa became a global icon for selfless service to others. Through her Missionaries of Charity, she personally cared for thousands of sick and dying people in Kolkata, India. She was the embodiment of empathy, equality and leading ethical practice, and showed that being humble and humane could challenge the status quo.

- **Greta Thunberg** (born 2003) is a Swedish environmental activist whose tireless campaigning has gained international recognition. Thunberg is known for her straightforward speaking manner – both in public and to political leaders and assemblies – in which she urges immediate action to address the global threat of climate change. She shows that passion is a driver for change, uses both facts and emotions to call out inaction, harnesses the power of strength in numbers to win attention, and gives children around the world a means of acting on climate change rather than just feeling anxious.

What do these examples have in common? What effects of these upstanders' work resonate with you, based on your own leadership or what you would like to achieve?

Upstander traits

Our accumulated strengths, passion, fears and experiences shape who we become. We grow by learning from others and from ourselves.

I have been able to view, analyse and define the following upstander traits by working with various companies and their workplace culture renovations. These are the key traits that make individuals powerful and important to workplaces, society and the world:

- **Courageous:** Taking a stand against what's wrong takes bravery, resilience and the perseverance to see things through no matter how big the obstacles appear. Courage comes more easily when your internal need to do the right thing is allowed to take precedence over fear and uncertainty. Courage involves speaking up when others do not. The effect is to galvanise people around you.

- **Vigilant:** Vigilance is about more than merely being observant; it's about constantly taking the pulse of the workplace climate and being fully aware of what's going on around you. It involves looking, listening and reading between the lines so you can anticipate problem areas and focus your attention and energy where it's most needed. Being vigilant comes down to four things: listening, asking the right questions, observing, and acting upon your discoveries when necessary. The effect is to explore and expose injustices.

- **Leader:** Leadership has nothing to do with position, authority or domination – it's about influence, respect, inspiration and showing the way. Upstanders distinguish themselves from silent bystanders by showing up, speaking up and leading by example. The best leaders value the ideas of others and are able to suppress their own personal agendas for the greater good. They're generous with their time and attention, placing the needs and concerns of their colleagues first. The effect is to role-model and demonstrate what's possible.

- **Principled:** Being principled means recognising the difference between right and wrong, and basing your actions on your morals. A principled upstander has an unwavering belief in always doing what's right in the face of injustice, every time. They possess a clear moral code that won't allow them to stand by and do nothing when a colleague is suffering. The effect is to foster justice, fairness, honesty and integrity.

- **Empathetic:** Empathy is an ability to put yourself in someone's shoes and try to understand their feelings and perceptions. Empathy is a habit that can be developed. It's different from kindness or pity. It's a mindset and an emotional direction that affirms that humans are wired for social cooperation and mutual aid. It's an awareness of suffering and a responsibility to act on that awareness. The effect is validation: people feel seen, heard and valued.

- **Emotionally Intelligent:** Many people are incredibly smart but lack the self-awareness, social skills or emotional savvy to maintain mature and beneficial interpersonal relationships. In contrast, an emotionally intelligent upstander excels at reading social situations and facilitating communication and motivation. This capacity to successfully balance cognition and emotion is contagious. The effect is support – helping work colleagues to manage their own feelings more effectively.

- **Initiator:** An initiator isn't afraid of new ideas. They're the first to embrace the untried, the unproven and the audacious. Upstanders are instigators of positivity, and creators of novel concepts and actions. They set the agenda. To them, the status quo only has value when it works. The effect is innovation: they're bold enough to take the reins of new habits, new policies and improved processes.

- **Self-reliant:** Self-reliance is one of the most powerful traits we can possess. With this weapon in our arsenal, we're able to take ownership of our own behaviour – good and bad. Our sense of self-worth and satisfaction doesn't depend on the random opinions of others. We understand that what happens to us is far less important than how we react to those events. We view failure as a useful stepping stone. The effect is resilience, which encourages others to bounce forward from setbacks.

- **Honest:** It's a sad fact that some people have a rubbery attitude toward honesty. They hedge their bets with half-truths, fudge their emotions with rationalisations, and lie to themselves and others. The Honest upstander, however, treats honesty as sacred. They are not afraid to speak out in the name of truth. They won't water down facts, embrace bias or edit reality. The effect is integrity, which helps everyone to maintain the highest standards.

Exercise: Total score

How many of these traits would you say you demonstrate? Give yourself one point for each of the nine you would say you possess:

- If you scored 8 to 9 points, you have an extraordinary level of upstander traits.
- If you scored 5 to 7 points, you have some upstander skills to build.
- If you scored 0 to 5 points, you have a lot of upstander skills to gain. That's okay – it's what this book is all about!

Understanding the upstander effect may be the most important knowledge you ever gain, and the most enriching. It is an undeniable fact that being a silent bystander in a world that needs courage doesn't make you feel good about yourself or allow you to leave the legacy you want to achieve. Understanding and harnessing the upstander effect is a powerful leadership strategy for success.

It's time to lead the change. Be an upstander leader. Stop hiding in the shadows – make your impact and have a lasting ripple effect.

You don't have to become a frontline worker to be an upstander. You don't have to frequently save cars full of girls from highway pile-ups. It can all start with a simple act – using your voice to be empathetic, courageous and compassionate.

Chapter 4

The upstander generation

We are at an interesting time in history as people become healthier and live longer, and therefore stay in the workforce longer. This is fascinating, as for the first time in history we have five generations working together.

For example, Joe Biden was elected President of the United States of America at 78 years old. Joe is part of the 'Silent Generation', which gained its name from its members living in the shadow of the much larger post –World War II generation. In fact, until Biden, no member of the Silent Generation had been elected US President.

Meanwhile, the oldest members of generation Z – five generations on – are 26 at the time of writing and are also in the workforce. So, if we have these generations now working together, how does this impact workplace culture and expectations, and how you lead?

What generation are you? Here are the seven living generations:

- The Greatest Generation (born 1901 to 1927)
- The Silent Generation (born 1928 to 1945)
- Baby boomers (born 1946 to 1964)
- Generation X (born 1965 to 1980)

- Generation Y, aka 'Millennials' (born 1981 to 1995)
- Generation Z (born 1996 to 2010)
- Generation alpha (born 2011 to 2025)

How many generations are currently working together in your workplace?

A topic that is on a lot of leaders' lips in the workshops that I run is the divide between these generations. Many people who are in senior positions within organisations – my client base – sit within the gen X and baby boomer generations. In my recent conversations with baby boomers, they have asked curious questions about how to manage millennials.

Millennials now make up about 35 per cent of workplaces, and that number is growing – it is expected to be 75 per cent by 2030. But studies are already showing that 43 per cent of millennials envision leaving their jobs within two years of being hired, and only 28 per cent seek to stay beyond five years. According to research, they are purpose-driven, enjoy self-guided work, believe in feedback and trust from leaders, and place a much higher value on integrity and ethics in the workplace than previous generations. I call them the 'upstander generation'. They are the most significant generation since the baby boomers – they are driving the future of business and creating a new working environment for generation Z (gen Z), generation alpha and so on.

With the advancement of technology, millennials and gen Z have access to more information than previous generations did at their age. As such, they have had access to the movement era: they're looking at #MeToo, BLM and March4Justice and understanding that they no longer need to put up with toxic behaviours.

While I spend a lot of time supporting millennials, I also talk to baby boomers and help educate them. Something that keeps cropping up is the common belief that a certain level of disrespect in the workplace is 'how it's done'. I hear comments like, 'When I was younger, this is how my boss treated me', or, 'Going on my experience within the construction industry, the apprentice was made fun of and made to do rituals to initiate them into the workforce'.

A common theme I share is that the dinosaur days are gone – those behaviours and that language are no longer something that we can support in the workplace. Just because something is how it has always been done, does that mean we should continue it, or is it our duty to break the cycle?

This is where millennials are paving the way – standing up, challenging the status quo and saying, 'We want respect in our workplaces and everywhere in our lives'.

Cultivating the upstander generation's passion

There's a lot of work to be done to bridge the gap between the upstander generation and baby boomers, but it requires understanding how different generations work. Millennials and gen Z want to feel valued, seen, heard and appreciated. They want to make sure that the work they're doing is having an impact, not just within the workplace but in the economy, the environment and the global community.

Why are millennials and gen Z different from previous generations? Israeli professor Yuval Noah Harari suggested in his book *Sapiens: A brief history of humankind* that 'a jumbo brain is a jumbo drain' and that humans' overly rapid evolution has caused our confidence to lag behind our intelligence, allowing doubt and existentialism to creep in.

If these were concepts that we as humanity already struggled with, what has the advancement of technology and our increased reliance upon it done to alter this? You guessed it: it has exacerbated the situation further.

As millennials and gen Z have been raised in this problematic environment, it seems only logical that they must change the environment to better suit modern humans. The upstander generation will seek to change environments proactively and for the benefit of all life.

Thankfully, some organisations are already adjusting to this. One of my clients, the CEO of Orange City Council, is passionate about this topic because he wants to create a generation of culture-driven upstanders. He wants to sustain them within the workplace and encourage them to stay, innovate and avoid just jumping into the global market due to boredom. He wants to develop them to have longevity, and for leadership positions at the council to be taken up by the next generation of leaders.

How can you harness your baby boomers to mentor and inspire the next generation of leaders and create a partnership approach? How can you harness the upstander generation for good within your organisation?

Busting the millennial and gen Z myths

At a workshop I ran in 2020, when I asked senior leaders about their biggest concerns surrounding workplace culture, one manager expressed confusion about acquiring the skills to effectively lead millennial and gen Z employees. She asked, 'What do they really want?'

Are they really a generation that feels overly privileged and wants everything served to them on a platter? This is a common myth I hear about millennials and gen Z, along with that they are work-shy and can't take feedback. But are these myths really true? Or are millennials and gen Z simply willing to rip up conventional wisdom when it comes to work, because they know it is possible to love what you do and where you work and still have an impact?

The workplace is currently split mostly between gen X and millennials, with each holding contrasting views and values in the workplace and misconceptions about one another's visions and goals. So, what are the common myths about millennials (and gen Z, who are entering the workforce now)?

· They have no work ethic.
· They are not prepared to put in the hours to get ahead.
· They have little respect for authority.
· They refuse to reach an expected level of maturity.

These are all easily debunked by understanding that, as time has passed, cultural and societal expectations have changed:

· Millennials and gen Z were raised in the 'intrapreneur era' and prefer to self-manage. An 'intrapreneur' is an inside entrepreneur, who uses their ideas to develop innovative products and services from within an organisation.
· For millennials and gen Z, jobs and careers are less a centre point for life and more a means to live a comfortable life.
· Millennials and gen Z believe that the primary prerequisites for respect are not age and experience but instead actions such as loyalty, trust, benevolence and passion.
· What is 'mature' is different for every generation. Two hundred years ago, it was expected that women would be married and starting a family at an age when we now expect them to still be at school and under the legal guardianship of their parents.

Leading the upstander generation – it's not that hard!

Leading this new and different generation does require changes, but the upstander generation welcomes changes. I often hear leaders say that it's difficult to manage millennials and gen Z, but what if you changed your mindset? Are they really difficult to manage, or do they simply expect more of you as a leader than you've been giving? I've seen amazingly harmonious and innovative workforces that consist largely of millennials and gen Z, working fluidly under a non-millennial leader. It just takes some forward-thinking strategies.

When it comes to leading the upstander generation, I have narrowed it down to five key points, drawing on firsthand feedback from millennial employees and business leaders:

1. Obtain
2. Explain
3. Train
4. Maintain
5. Retain

Obtain

When recruiting millennials and gen Z, understand that they are less focused on big salary bundles and more on the look, feel and vibe of an organisation. Culture is key. When millennials and gen Z are scanning the marketplace for their next job, how their potential employer portrays the overall experience of working for them is crucial.

Tip: Express the culture you currently have, and outline how you wish to improve it and what kind of employee you are looking for to aid this change. Millennials and gen Z respect openness and honesty, and are eager to be a part of change.

Explain

Millennials and gen Z (and indeed all staff) want open and honest communication. They are brutally honest with each other, and they expect the same from their employer. They want to feel as though their opinion matters, and that their insights are contributing to a bigger picture that is allowing the company to develop.

Companies need to adopt a transparent communication policy. For example, they might want to host a weekly drop-in session with the leadership team, where even the most junior staff can pose questions to the C-suite executives. Something that worked very well in my last role was closing the feedback loop: making 360-degree feedback the norm means that millennials and gen Z not only receive honest feedback on a regular basis but are also empowered to dole it out.

Tip: Business leaders should walk about the office and build relationships on a deeper level. Create an open-door policy within and between teams.

Train

Growth and personal development are key. Millennials and gen Z want mentoring; companies need to consider how they are going to provide mentoring to 50 per cent of their workforce, and fast. Introducing mentoring programmes early on for millennials and gen Z who have just started in their jobs gives them hope from the outset that their employer truly prioritises their development.

Millennials and gen Z crave knowledge. They're used to having information at their fingertips and thrive on processing it. (The jumbo brain is growing with technology and must be fed!) In short, if they're not learning, they're not developing – and if they're not developing, then they're going to start looking for a way out.

Companies need to prioritise learning and, more importantly, upgrade how it happens. Millennials and gen Z don't want formal lectures or a bunch of data hitting them in the face all at once. KPMG did well by offering three-year learning paths to provide technical, business and soft-skill confidence delivered via a blended, flexible approach. It offers snackable learning options that are easy to get in and out of – continuous but also relaxed. Leveraging modern technology that millennials and gen Z know and love through e-learning makes a huge difference – why not deliver training via podcast, video, Slack or the team's social channel? It conveys a message that work should be a natural and relaxed part of life.

COVID-19 has, of course, accelerated this leveraging of modern technology. Allow this change in your work environment to reinvent ways of communication and training to better suit the bulk of your workforce.

Tip: Check out Upstand Academy. A keynote is brilliant for setting the tone and getting a short burst of motivation and awareness of key issues going on within the workplace – but it normally stops there. We have built an ongoing digital curriculum providing a hybrid learning experience that doesn't stop after the keynote is finished. Three-, six- and twelve-month learning journeys are available to your team, on our platform or yours.

Maintain

Millennials and gen Z need the right manager. After all, people don't leave a company, they leave a bad manager. They need a leader who celebrates wins and small successes, and encourages growth from failure. Millennials and gen Z are now increasingly hoping for gratitude for small-scale successes that might usually be overlooked. While big project milestones are generally celebrated, they also want to feel as though their day-to-day efforts are being noticed.

Millennials and gen Z are purpose-driven leaders who believe in social causes. In a World Economic Forum study surveying 5000 millennials across 18 countries, respondents said that the top overall priority for any business should be 'to improve society'. Therefore, millennials and gen Z are likely to opt into opportunities to work and grow through social impact initiatives.

Tip: Consider rewards and recognition schemes, and peer-on-peer recognition (and gratitude). In my experience, developing a process for individuals to recognise peers for great work is fantastic for team culture. Usually rewards and recognition come from the top and can feel icky, but peers recognising peers is a powerful gesture that feels authentic and genuine.

Retain

Millennials and gen Z demand balance and flexibility. Companies need to ingrain flexibility to foster an 'anytime, anywhere' work environment to replace the traditional nine-to-five mentality. Opportunities such as being able to work from home one or more days a week, or being able to take time out from the working day to deal with personal commitments, are huge benefits. Millennials and gen Z want security in their work, but also the knowledge that they are not trapped in their work.

Tip: Foster open communication about alternate ways of working that break from the nine-to-five mentality. Every workplace is different – see what works for you.

Summary

The number-one expectation millennials and gen Z have today is that employers will provide respect, trust and open communication as well as demand it. For too long, workers have chosen a job and accepted the culture it fosters despite disagreeing with it, because at least it was a secure job. Millennials and gen Z are not willing to stand for inappropriate behaviour that doesn't belong in the workplace, because they can just leave. Quitting a job because of bad culture is not synonymous with an inability to withstand banter, but is instead a recognition that workplace bullying is not acceptable and does not have to be tolerated.

The workforce is now so broad that you no longer need to choose one job that you will stick to for life, in which you must obey your employer's every rule (even when unethical and toxic) for fear of not finding another job. Millennials and gen Z are realising this and are not standing for leaders who are unwilling to accept and encourage change.

To lead millennials and gen Z successfully and tap into their upstanding qualities, these are the main points to focus upon (I promise it'll be worth it!):

· Invest in training and development for all leaders. Creating a healthy culture starts from the top.
· Discuss the elephant in the room of bullying and harassment, and deal with it. Be proactive in preventing it – let's leave behind the days when complaints were swept under the rug.
· Be adaptable and agile, and value remote learning and working – check out the Upstand Academy.
· Encourage innovation and build intrapreneurs.
· Incorporate reward and recognition into your employees' lives.
· Encourage social impact initiatives, such as being green and recycling.
· Value diversity and new norms.

Chapter 5

The upstander and bystander zones

This chapter is about understanding more deeply the reasons why people in the workplace fail to speak up for their peers. For many years, and as the founder of Bullyology and the Upstand Academy, I've been fascinated by the many reasons why workplace bystanders may or may not choose to speak up. Over time, I've come to recognise that everyone in the workplace falls into at least one of four clearly defined zones (and those who fall into more than one zone are usually in a transition phase from bystander to upstander). The first three zones – the Uncomfortable Zone, the Unconscious Zone and the Avoidance Zone – are the bystander zones, and are unhelpful and often harmful. Meanwhile, the fourth zone – the Upstander Zone – can be a powerful catalyst for change (see Figure 1).

Understanding these zones is critical in ensuring that you have a healthy company culture in which people feel able to contribute their ideas, be themselves and speak up. In a bystander culture, you may see an increase in sickness, absence, stress and team misalignment, as well as higher staff turnover, which can be a huge financial detriment to your organisation. More significant than high staff turnover, however, having a bystander culture can impact your organisation's reputation and your personal reputation, which causes lasting damage that is hard to recover from.

Figure 1: The four zones

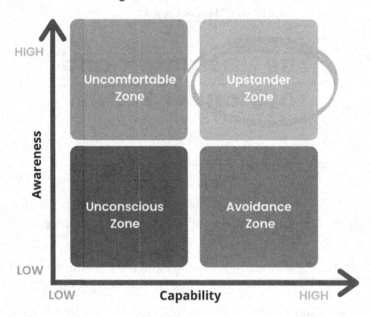

For the last four years, I've been having daily discussions with people in various teams, organisations and industries in order to discover the core reason why some people fall into the bystander zones. In one workshop, during a group discussion, three leaders explained some of the reasons why they chose to bystand instead of upstand.

One said, 'I was totally oblivious to what was going on right under my nose. I guess I was too caught up in my own ego in my first leadership role. I was focused on my own success, and I didn't understand that success was a team sport'. This is, of course, a clear and common example of the Unconscious Zone.

The second leader said, 'I did know it was going on and I didn't like it, but I didn't know how to stop the bullying and harassment or where to seek help'. This leader, unlike the first one, had awareness but was uncomfortable with her capability to respond to the situation, placing her in the Uncomfortable Zone.

The third leader was a perfect example of a bystander in the Avoidance Zone, claiming that, 'To be honest, I think that it's not my problem. I lead the team and look after the trade element of the business. I think that the people problem is still a HR issue'.

Later that week, I was reflecting on the conversations and confessions that I had witnessed and decided to start thinking about the bystander and upstander zones I am presenting in this chapter. I had spent a lot of time reading Amy C. Edmondson's book *The Fearless Organisation* and exploring her psychological safety zones, which inspired me to delve into the bystander zones.

Leaders have a duty of care. The more you lean in and understand how these bystander zones can impact your company's culture, the better you can become as a leader. Otherwise, you risk allowing toxic behaviours to take hold of your organisational culture, ultimately ruining employee, business and personal success.

Let's go into the details of each of these zones, and see why they are so prevalent and how you may be falling into them.

The Unconscious Zone

The Unconscious Zone is characterised by a low level of awareness about the work climate you are operating in. It's a case of 'what you don't know can't hurt you'. A common symptom of being in this zone is being unfamiliar with the bystander effect. As we discussed in chapter 2, the bystander effect basically means that the more people that are available to solve a particular problem, the less likely any given individual will bother to take action. It's the old 'someone else will probably fix it' mindset, and the common result is that no one ever speaks up. Unacceptable behaviours and unsafe or unproductive practice become normalised.

Have you ever noticed how otherwise intelligent people can become unobservant, ignorant or biased about a particular situation or behaviour happening around them? This is known as 'blind spot syndrome'. The classic example is when a toxic manager with limited social or communication skills, a fragile ego and a 'my way or the highway' leadership style negatively impacts the wellbeing and productivity of those equal to them or within their team. Despite the fact that everyone else in the office is aware of this individual's shortcomings and toxic behaviours, management appears to be totally oblivious.

These blind spots within a business can stem from cynicism, lopsided social pecking orders or the formation of in-groups, subgroups and subcultures.

In-groups are groups of people who identify as belonging together. They naturally lead to the creation of out-groups – people who are identified as not belonging. In-groups and out-groups are often formed through unconscious bias or preconceived notions. Sub-grouping, meanwhile, is a normal process that can occur with a larger group, and can be either helpful or harmful. Subcultures can form based on business unit, geography, job type or position, department or industry; they can form wherever people interact regularly, and can be based on something as simple as start times or smoking breaks.

There is an emphasis on self-protection above the psychological health of the workplace and team. When a person in a company is perceived as too valuable to lose or someone who can do no wrong, it becomes easier for the upper ranks to ignore how drastically harmful that person is to the wellbeing of the workplace.

Take my bully as an example. He was highly confident in his role with regard to industrial relations and hiring and firing people, but when it came to people skills, he was absolutely awful – he was detrimentally controlling and coercive. The higher-ups kept him in the organisation because he was able to be productive for them – a selfish act.

Another example is a sales executive at an organisation I worked with. Sometimes the competitive nature of a sales environment can cause toxicity within the team. This person was an extraordinary sales candidate but a highly toxic influence on the team. I kept hearing, 'But they're very good at their job. They close deals'.

As a leader, I want you to acknowledge that one reason why people become bystanders and ignore toxic behaviours is because often the people displaying those behaviours are highly competent or skilled at their job; but this is not an excuse for ignorance.

In order to address poor workplace culture, we must first be able to pick up on the clues that it exists. Being alert, observant, proactive and fully in tune with the social dynamics of a workplace gives us a head start in dealing with the problems that arise because we can see them coming ahead of time. If we're wrapped up in our own tasks, goals and emotions, we can often fail to notice what's transpiring in the workplace more broadly. We can't offer much insight into negative issues if we don't know they exist. This is the unconscious bias that develops and hinders movement out of the Unconscious Zone.

Put simply, unconscious bias is the personal bias that happens without conscious awareness. We make associations and develop preferences in various social categories – gender, age, disability, race, social status, sexuality – without necessarily being aware we're doing it. Unconscious biases can lead to the automatic stereotyping of certain individuals or groups and have a negative effect on workplace diversity and inclusion.

Examples of unconscious bias in the workplace are common. Have you ever worked with or hired someone who reminded you of another person? It's subtle, but still a form of unconscious bias. Effective leaders have the ability to put aside past experiences and see people as individuals. (This can be difficult at times, so leaders should feel comfortable asking for others' input.) Recently, I had a client tell me they didn't trust a staff member because he reminded her of an ex-partner who was untrustworthy. She made comments such as, 'There is just something about them'. But from an outsider's perspective, this is obviously not a strong enough reason to warrant isolating this person.

Exercise: Beating your bias

Battling our own unconscious biases is never easy. This is why training is so important. Targeted training can teach us how to chip away at them so their impact can be minimised. We must learn to be more self-aware. How are your actions – or lack of action – influencing your overall work environment? Can you think of any unconscious biases you may have?

The Uncomfortable Zone

People in the Uncomfortable Zone have a high level of awareness of what's happening in their workplace. Unfortunately, this is coupled with insufficient resources and training. It's not that they're ignorant of the problem – they're ignorant of the solution. Leaders and employees have no clue about what steps to take when problems arise. There may be minimal safety protocols, a complete lack of clarity on behaviour or expectations, or zero management training on how to deal with negative work issues appropriately, safely and effectively. A lack of easy-to-understand and easy-to-implement processes leads to confusion and overwhelmed employees who become reluctant to address bullying, harassment, employee mental health, discrimination and similar issues.

When leaders don't know how to listen, when employees feel more comfortable ignoring issues than speaking up and asking questions, when staff are deadly afraid to admit a mistake, when valuable voices are drummed out and when going against the status quo is perceived as intrusive and disruptive, the problem often boils down to inadequate training and capability. Either leaders aren't aware of the deep level of training available, or they choose not to invest in that training. It can also result from businesses not taking the time to create clear expectations and procedures, or outline a consistent, workable response. This can often result in business leaders like yourself incorrectly assuming that they can solve problems on the fly, not realising the damage that has already been done to the business.

When employees and managers don't have the tools, resources, education or training to deal with these issues, the road to profitability in a healthy workplace becomes paved with obstacles. Anxiety levels rise and efficiency plummets. Solutions for repairing or preventing damage to reputation, employee health and wellbeing, and profit margins need to be ongoing and consistent.

Research shows that when consumers witness or are made aware of toxicity directed at an employee within the workplace, they can develop negative opinions that steer them away from purchasing from that company or business. The survey found that employees who have experienced an unfair workplace will even actively discourage potential customers from purchasing products or services from their employer. As a leader, can you afford for this to happen?

In my experience of working in a toxic environment, my colleagues were extremely uncomfortable – and so was I – for a long period of time. Aside from the bullying, there were other comments that, looking back, I realised were toxic. I remember a manager winking and making a comment one day about my tan while in an open-plan office. 'Ooh, you've got a tan. Have you tanned your white bits as well?' I was shocked and giggled to pass it off, then walked away from the situation. (Have you ever noticed yourself giggle or laugh awkwardly in response to a 'joke' or banter? I have found, on reflection, that I have done this when I feel extremely uncomfortable about a comment directed at me, such as in this example.) I also saw some of my colleagues look down and awkwardly dismiss the comment.

This comment was extremely inappropriate and constitutes sexual harassment in the workplace. Sexual harassment is behaviour categorised by the making of unwelcome and inappropriate sexual remarks or physical advances in the workplace, or in other professional or social situations.

Bullying or banter?

Another issue that is often ignored in toxic workplaces is the difference between bullying and banter. Often when inappropriate comments are called out in the workplace, they are met with a response such as, 'Toughen up', or, 'It's only banter', or, 'It's a joke, don't be so sensitive'. All of these are comments I've personally heard. I find it fascinating how often I hear 'It's just banter' in different environments, and especially male-dominated environments.

Dealing with this issue starts with understanding the definition of 'bullying' versus 'banter'. Bullying is intentional, harmful, persistent and typically involves a power imbalance. It sets out to make a person feel worse about themselves. Banter, on the other hand, is a playful exchange of teasing remarks. It's mutually good-natured, grounded and friendly. As an example, my childhood best friend and I call each other nicknames that we developed when we were younger, which are comfortable because we have a mutual exchange; but if someone else called me by this nickname, it wouldn't be the same and it wouldn't be funny.

Scan your workplace environment and identify some of the comments you hear. Make a conscious decision as to whether they are bullying or banter.

During your career, you may have experienced someone nit-picking at your insecurities, making comments about your height or appearance, or generalising about your race. Often these things slip under the radar and can be passed off as banter. It's up to you to make a conscious decision whether these comments are bullying or banter. Do you feel uncomfortable? Also, if someone needs to look over their shoulder to check if someone's listening before they make a comment, that comment is not acceptable in the workplace (or anywhere).

Exercise: Banter check

Reflect on your own workplace and leadership. When is a joke or banter acceptable? When might you need to intervene as a leader? Can you reflect on a time when 'banter' made you feel uncomfortable?

The Avoidance Zone

Some people are incredibly good at distancing themselves from office dramas. Their philosophy is, 'If it doesn't affect me personally and directly, then I'm not interested'. This selfish, ultra-safe approach may seem to work for a short while, but when one person in the workplace fails to speak up about safety, wellbeing and unfairness, the entire business ultimately suffers.

Lacking awareness or not feeling able to act due to a lack of training is one thing, but it is even more awkward and soul-destroying when those in a position to make a difference choose to ignore the toxic behaviours they see happening in their workplace. It reminds me of a toddler who tightly covers their eyes and assumes that because they can't see you, you can't possibly see them either. They ignore the problem and hope it goes away. This approach hurts everyone and almost never works. Tossing the problem in the too-hard basket erodes trust in leadership, and employees begin to question the integrity and motivation of their colleagues and those in charge.

Avoidance isn't just a leadership issue. It's common for employees to develop a fear of the implemented hierarchy and become reluctant to report issues to their superior. They may fear retaliation or view such a bold action as unthinkable. They might not speak up because they want to fit in and be accepted by their peers, colleagues and leaders. They might be wary of being the bearer of bad news, afraid of the shoot-the-messenger mindset that some organisations foster. They may be discouraged by an anti-snitch culture in which the act of reporting someone else for wrongdoing is viewed negatively. Words such as 'dobber', 'rat', 'tattletale' or 'whistleblower' aren't favourable labels to get yourself. In some cases, people believe that whatever concerns they may have, the effort of speaking up about them isn't worth it – their voice won't be heard, the issue won't be addressed and nothing will ever change.

This sad situation is one of the prime indicators of a toxic work environment in which employees have given up all hope in their leaders. Leaders have diminished their trust. Staff and management hang out in the Avoidance Zone for self-protection because it suits their goals and agendas. Their solution is to evade, distract, dismiss, pacify, and only take actions that maintain their own comfort levels. I've seen leaders sidestep responsibility, hoping issues will magically go away by themselves. They know there's a problem and have the solution to fix that problem, but they choose to dodge it.

Employees are less likely to remain in a toxic workplace environment. Recent research by HR.com and EVERFI shows that employee turnover is one of the largest impacts of toxic work environments. Also, replacing those leaving staff members can prove equally problematic. A survey uncovered that 58 per cent of respondents who witnessed unfairness in the workplace in the last year would discourage potential employees from joining the company.

When I was subjected to a prolonged period of workplace bullying at the hands of my direct manager, I discovered how far the avoidance mindset could (and often does) go. It became entrenched and habitual. My thirty-plus complaints about the atrociously unfair behaviour were met with temporary fixes, briefly distancing me from my bully, moving me between departments, endless false promises such as, 'We will certainly look into it', and dismissive disinterest: 'It's a personality clash. You're tough. You're confident. Just ignore him'. This avoidance was ultimately so damaging that it eventually led to me winding up in a hospital bed.

While writing this chapter, a horrific news story landed in my social media feed, and I couldn't help but scream 'Avoidance! Avoidance! Avoidance!' in my head. A woman was allegedly sexually assaulted on a train in Philadelphia, but despite there being a number of witnesses, they all failed to stop the incident or call the police. As a result of this avoidance, a second alleged rape then occurred on the same train line. Upper Darby Police Department Superintendent Timothy Bernhardt commented, 'Anybody that was on that train has to look in the mirror and ask why they didn't intervene or why they didn't do something'.

Exercise: Avoiding avoidance

What feelings arose in you when reading that story? Time and time again, we see people in the Avoidance Zone demonstrate the bystander effect and fail to intervene in acts of criminality or toxicity.

The Upstander Zone

Of the four zones, the Upstander Zone is the one to aspire to. This is where the transformational work happens. Leaders who sift through unconscious, uncomfortable and avoidant workplace behaviours can radically change business outcomes for the better. The upstander is a bystander no more.

An upstander is a positive change maker and a beacon of light who never fails to speak up when faced with injustice and negativity. An upstander lives in a constant state of readiness to stand up for what's fair and just. They are attuned to the social pulse of the workplace, using their emotional intelligence to keep on top of office dynamics and support those who need help and encouragement the most.

Those in the Upstander Zone carry around a full toolkit of empathy, ethics, equality, elite communication, and professional and personal integrity – and the right level of training and capability. They firmly believe that every voice in the workplace matters, and the business only thrives when everyone is heard, seen, valued and supported. I have seen time and time again how much change a single upstander can create in the workplace. Now imagine what it would be like to have everyone in your team and organisation living comfortably in the Upstander Zone.

Someone who comes up frequently in my workshops as an example of an upstander is Grace Tame, an Australian advocate for survivors of sexual assault. Grace was named Australian of the Year in 2021. As someone who shared her own personal story to inspire others to speak up and share theirs, she is a prime example of someone who sits in the Upstander Zone. This is encapsulated in her tweet that said, 'Perpetrators and their apologies will do the worst. We're not afraid. We just have to keep doing our best. And we will. We'll keep sharing, listening and working with all those who are willing.

We'll remain open and inclusive and hopeful, but we will never ever surrender the good fight'.

Exercise: Zone shift

What zone are you in presently? How about the majority of your team or organisation? What would need to change? What role could you play in this?

How is your speak-up culture?

In an accountable, psychologically safe workplace, the big culture question is this: how comfortable do employees feel in voicing their most pressing concerns? In other words, is your workplace speak-up friendly? Here are a few ways to tell if it is:

- All staff feel free to ask questions, raise issues and express informal opinions.
- Leaders welcome all input, whether positive, negative or neutral.
- CEOs, managers and employees can agree to disagree without bitterness and revenge.
- Employees are confident they can speak up without retaliation.
- Lively debate, including disagreement, is welcome and encouraged.
- Employees feel a sense of responsibility to raise issues and concerns.
- There's a system in place for anonymous upstanding or old-school whistleblowing when appropriate.
- Employees' input is valued by management and leadership, whether it is implemented or not.
- It is clear that listening to staff concerns is a major priority across the business.

- When action is required in response to employee concerns, there's a confident expectation that it will be decisive, fair and carefully considered.

When the emotional culture is strong, the professional culture will follow. When all employees feel genuinely connected, they're more engaged and work outcomes are improved. Anxiety and confusion are replaced with confidence, team pride and a joy of belonging. That is something truly special.

When you have a good speak-up culture, it won't just be up to you to identify what zone your team sits within – you can have an open, frequent dialogue where feedback is collective. People will be comfortable to chat and provide information. You can more clearly check the pulse of your team's psychological safety.

I've seen this done very well when I was part of a team, and also when working with multiple organisations and clients. They have a 'safety share' or a 'safety moment' before each meeting. Leaders initiate this by discussing what went wrong, what their role entailed that week, any lessons learned, and any challenges or thought patterns that are holding them back. By having an open forum to check in before each meeting, a vulnerability shift can take place. Through leaders modelling this behaviour, employees can feel comfortable to speak up in real time. Provide space to have open discussions and team check-ins, and give your team members the opportunity to disagree with one another.

Transparency can increase by enrolling colleagues to do follow-ups on their own lessons learned through sharing and learning from one another. This creates psychological safety. Having workers speak up in real time to the person in power allows a strong cultural shift. After all, a conversation can save a life.

How is the speak-up culture within your team and workplace? Do you address the elephant in the room, or do toxic behaviours tend to get pushed under the dusty rug? Do you, as a leader, demonstrate vulnerability by sharing your own lessons learned, mistakes and challenges? Do you then help others to do the same?

If you have identified that you sit within the Unconscious Zone, the Uncomfortable Zone or the Avoidance Zone, be kind to yourself. You are brave. You are on this journey with me. Awareness is the first step to building capability and change as a leader. You need to reflect on where your team currently sits and assess how you can elevate upstander capability and awareness. Examine your workplace environment and make a conscious leadership commitment to create cultural change.

Chapter 6

The new age – empathy, ethics and equality

Earlier, I explained the values and inspiration behind the Upstander movement – a movement for global change and great leadership that changes with the times and looks to the future for solutions. Then I delved into the problem with bystanders who ignore and avoid problems. We looked at the nine archetypes of bystander behaviour and which may apply to you. We discussed how the solution is to apply the upstander effect, to shift bystanders out of their three destructive zones and into the upstander zone.

Now, we need to understand what the prime conditions are for the Upstander movement to occur in your workplace. The answer is the three Es: empathy, ethics and equality.

In this chapter we explore how the three Es are fundamental to business survival (see Figure 2), especially in this new age of change in which the value of empathy, ethics and equality are on the rise in the workplace. I will clearly define each of these values and outline why they are fundamental for upstander leaders.

If you connect all of the ideas that we've explored so far, you will see why the three Es are so important. We are in an age in which toxic stories are being called out to ignite a more hopeful, purpose-driven and human-centred future. I call this a new age of empathy, ethics and equality. As we have discussed in previous chapters, workplace leadership has changed over the decades – authoritarian rules, protected hierarchies and emotional distance have given way to the realisation that the most productive workforce is a happy and openly communicative one. True leadership is the ability to transform ego into contribution and create meaningful connections in the workplace. As a leader, you must embed a solid foundation of empathy, ethics and equality at the core of your company and community DNA.

Figure 2: The three Es

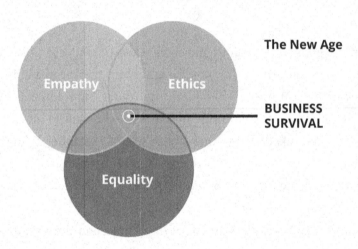

Fostering the three Es will allow a positive culture to grow with much less effort on your part as a leader. By instilling empathy, ethics and equality into the bedrock of organisational culture, you can create teams infused with high levels of adaptability and resilience. This, in turn, prepares them to thrive now and into the future.

I learned to ride a bike around the age of four or five. At first, like many kids, I started with training wheels and guidance. Over time, it became a natural habit that didn't need much thought or attention. The three Es, over time and with dedication and commitment, become easy and as natural as riding a bike.

On one occasion, I remember crashing my bike into the back of a parked truck. The crash threw me over the handlebars and I hit the back of the truck. I had the scrapes and bruises on my face to show it. Don't get me wrong, at first we need some guidance even with training wheels, but over time the three Es become second nature and embedded into our personal and company DNA. Just like riding a bike, practice makes perfect.

A collective awareness and understanding of the three Es is required to protect your workplace's biggest assets – its people. From this, your organisation can grow.

Understanding empathy

Empathy, like resilience, isn't something you're born with – it's something you develop and build upon as you go through life. Think of empathy as being thoughtful and supportive. It's the ability to understand and share someone else's feelings. We do this by imagining what it would be like to experience their situation, seeing the world through their eyes. We want and choose to work with people who can do this, and they often emerge as natural leaders regardless of title or position.

According to Daniel Goleman's 2013 article in the *Harvard Business Review*, there are three distinct types of empathy. The first is cognitive empathy, which is the ability to understand another person's perspective. To be a strong leader is to learn how to step inside another person's shoes and see the world from their perspective. It's different from sympathy, which is feeling sorry for them. It involves using language to encourage others to share their perspective, such as, 'Help me understand', or 'How does that feel for you?' As Goleman points out, you must use language that the other person understands and that is meaningful to them; explanations are 'a skill essential to getting the performance from direct reports'.

As a leader, when I had to help someone who had been bullied, I practised cognitive empathy. This involved thinking about their feelings rather than feeling them myself, which might traumatise me and give me an unconscious bias towards their perspective of the situation.

Goleman points out that cognitive empathy is also about self-awareness: 'The executive circuits that allow us to think about our own thoughts and to monitor the feelings that flow from them let us apply the same reasoning to other people's minds when we choose to direct our attention that way'. I will talk more about self-awareness in the next chapter.

Goleman's second type of empathy is emotional empathy, or the ability to feel what someone else feels. 'It springs from ancient parts of the brain … that allow us to feel fast without thinking deeply'. It mirrors others' emotional states within our own bodies. I've experienced this with my family – it's hard for me not to feel deep emotional empathy if they're going through a hard time. Perhaps you've experienced this too. I also tend to mirror my husband's emotions.

This type of empathy is useful as it allows me to be present in the feeling, but it can be counterproductive if not managed with self-awareness. For example, if you mirror overemotional states at play in the workplace, you risk becoming a bystander or reacting in an unconscious or avoidant manner. I had a client whose child was being bullied, and it was hard for her not to become emotionally overinvolved, feel the feelings her child was going through and react from an emotional state.

Finally, Goleman defines a third empathy – empathetic concern, which is the ability to sense what another person needs from you. Empathetic concern 'is closely related to emotional empathy, [and] enables you to sense not just how people feel but what they need from you'. As an example, when I talk to my GP or therapist, I expect them to combine their science-backed expertise with an empathetic concern for my wellbeing to determine what I need to help me improve.

Here's another example, if you have a deep relationship with your colleagues or team, over time you develop the ability to notice the signs of when someone is feeling emotional, fatigued or overwhelmed. It can be a tricky balance to stay calm and help without pushing someone away by being too emotionally involved.

Why do we need empathy to become upstanders? The whole purpose of upstander leadership is to care about what is happening to others. Communication and understanding are key to any decision made or action taken in the workplace. We can make decisions sensibly if we are aware of our needs and those of our colleagues.

Every worker has different desires and expectations of their career, and it is their right to have these desires supported by colleagues and leaders. It is also essential, particularly in times of hardship, to recognise when other workers are struggling. This won't always be obvious, and it will require an understanding of each other. Empathy needs to be present in the workplace so that problems such as miscommunication, isolation and bullying can be prevented.

What causes empathy to be neglected?

It's time to bring up a term that has been making the rounds recently: toxic masculinity. Toxic masculinity is a set of attitudes and ways of behaving that are stereotypically associated with or expected of men, despite having negative impacts on society as a whole, no matter your gender. Toxic masculinity is the enemy of empathy. I was running a workshop in 2021 and a few men in the room began discussing empathy as a term related to women, with it being soft and fluffy. Realistically, it's an intrinsic human trait that allows us to connect; however, these men did not see it this way.

The notion that men in leadership positions should be tough, strong and independent, and hide their emotions, has led us away from understanding the necessity of empathy. It creates a competitive environment in which challenging the status quo is almost unheard of, and leads towards a culture in which it is okay to believe that the boss's decision is final, no matter who is negatively affected and how ethically wrong it might be. This is what an upstander leader needs to be aware of and move away from.

The assumption that men are not expected to be empathetic is damaging for everyone. When empathy is seen as weak, and attempts to understand other workers – especially from a leadership position – are viewed as incompetence or over-friendliness, team members of all genders are negatively impacted. Women in particular often counterproductively feel that they have to adopt a masculine energy to be given promotions and to have their opinions and ideas validated. In my case, my bully told me that my empathetic approach was making me seem soft and easy, and people would take advantage of my kindness. At times this resulted in me becoming a bystander to rude and offensive jokes, allowing toxic masculinity and sexist comments to slip by.

The dinosaur days of leaders needing to be selfish and stubborn are on their way out, and the new age of empathy, ethics and equality is being brought in. Men and women should be allowed to be equally strong, vulnerable and empathetic without fear of judgement and ridicule.

Have you observed these toxic, stereotypical assumptions in your workplace?

So, how can you incorporate empathy into your life?

To incorporate empathy into your life, be active in your curiosity about other people. You don't have the right to demand the thoughts, emotions and experiences of every stranger you meet, but by growing your curiosity, you can expand your knowledge and understanding of the people around you and become able to communicate far better.

With improved communication, you may find yourself learning, changing and growing for the better. Often over time, as you hone your empathetic skills, you can stop connecting empathy with the bad situations it relates to and simply learn from and understand the emotions objectively. You empathise with someone to help them through something. Empathy is beneficial for all parties – most importantly, you.

You first have to be active in your communication, which is based on observation and listening. The steps to becoming an upstander that are laid out in Part III will aid you in this.

Open up. You can hardly expect to understand others without letting them understand you, or even letting you understand yourself first. Empathy requires reflection and understanding of your own experiences and emotions. It is important to take time to do this. Think about why people act or think the way they do, or why someone might think the opposite of you. Open up to others and you may find that you will learn more about yourself as well.

Here are three specific ways to grow your empathy muscle:

1. When you ask people, 'How are you?' try to get past the simple answer. Repeat the question and really care about the answer. 'No, really, how are you?' By showing that your question is a quest to truly understand how they feel, you open up a whole range of possibilities for meaningful sharing.
2. Listen carefully and with your body. One of the best ways to build trust for someone is to match their breathing rate and body language, including facial expressions and vocal tone. It's almost like syncing your emotions to theirs in real time. Try it. It's surprisingly effective and can create instant rapport.

3. Play the 'walk a mile in their shoes' game. Notice some random person and imagine you are one of those science-fiction shapeshifters who can snap their fingers and magically become the other person. What would it be like to wear their clothes, have their face and body, and go through their day? Feel their emotions and experiences. View the world through their eyes.

The key to empathy is imagination. These exercises will stretch your empathy muscles by sending you into unfamiliar territory and places.

Ethics

I was asked once at a workshop what exactly constituted 'ethics', and it occurred to me that perhaps it was more complicated than it first seems. I define ethics as a set of values in which we question, understand and argue our opinions and beliefs. Our ethics are often deeply rooted within us. Like attitudes, our core ethics can sometimes be difficult to understand, and change as we grow. We often find ourselves defining who we are by our choices and our actions, which are inevitably driven by our ethics, so going against them is challenging.

Have you ever found yourself changing to fit in at work? While ethics are essential in the workplace, and must be demonstrated appropriately, there is still room for individual ideas from each person.

Leaders with empathy will encourage and demonstrate understanding of other people's ethics. It is important to demonstrate a proactive understanding of other people's ethics, which you may not share but can appreciate and respect. In my experience, ethics are the main contributor to our decision-making in upstander organisations. They play a part in our everyday life, particularly our work life, so we must develop a basis upon which we can understand our own and others' ethical standpoints and respect those that we do not share.

For example, I remember when I was younger, kids would steal candy from the store, but even at that age I had an ethical understanding that it was wrong, so I decided not to join in. Working as a council youth leader early in my career, I quickly established that not all youths understand stealing as ethically wrong, because they grew up in an environment where stealing was a way of life.

You, as a leader, need to have strong ethics that you abide by and enforce. Ethics can be taught. It's important to acknowledge that everyone has different values and beliefs, but you need to educate your team in the important ethics that form the bedrock of your organisation and get them on board. Ethics are invisible, so it is through having conversations about ethics that you can create alignment and understanding.

The choice to make ethical or unethical decisions in the workplace will directly correlate with the level of strain placed on every employer and employee, as well as on the relationships within the company and the growth of the company. Often, the outcomes of our decisions at work not only risk our reputation but the entire business's reputation.

A focus on ethical conduct should be paramount in ensuring your personal and business success. If you choose to ignore ethics at work and don't enforce the company's core ethics, your team will feel that the company's ethics don't sit right with them, and this can cause long-term damage. If someone on your team doesn't agree with the ethics of your team or organisation, are they really the right fit for your organisation? This is especially true if you are laying a foundation for an upstanding organisation.

There are many ways to encourage upstanding and respect of ethical conduct, but they all begin with an open team that is comfortable, honest and uplifting. Reflecting on the upstander generation discussed in chapter 4, let's explore how you can create a healthy work team that respects one another's ethics.

From my experience working with millennials, the number-one expectation I have seen is that they want employers who provide respect, trust and open communication. For too long, workers chose a job and just accepted the culture it fostered despite disagreeing with it; they stayed silent and became bystanders, too focused on the mentality of having a secure job for life. Millennials and gen Z are not willing to stand for inappropriate behaviour that doesn't belong in the workplace because they can just leave.

Quitting a job because of bad culture does not go hand in hand with an inability to withstand banter, but instead with a recognition that workplace bullying is not accepted and will not be tolerated. It's about having an ethical standpoint and sticking to it – both to attract the right talent and to retain the talent you already have.

We know through empathy why and how we can begin to embrace others. How can we understand and apply ethics in our workplace? Ethics is about questioning your first thought and coming up with a better one that is centred on your values and beliefs.

Exercise: Ethics check

Ask yourself these questions when you make a decision at work:

- Would I be happy and proud if this project or task was carried out under my name?
- Do I agree with this and feel comfortable with it?
- Is this choice unfairly favouring a group or an individual?
- Is this choice unfairly favouring me?
- Will this decision create a better workplace?
- Does this decision make anyone unnecessarily uncomfortable?

Workplaces are not always the easiest places to make difficult decisions that hurt no one, but ensuring that your decisions abide by your ethics and trusting that your core ethics are inclusive will mean that your decision-making becomes much fairer and much less stressful.

Equality

Equality means giving people equal chances, choices and opportunities, no matter who they are. It is often confused with equity – giving everyone the same things from different starting points, which does not allow them to finish in the same place. My experience with youth work showed me that not everyone has the same start to life. Some of us are born with advantages that we may not even recognise, as they are innately part of our experiences. Some of us are born with disadvantages, such as having little money or education, or being raised by abusive parents with little or no care and love. I had a crash course in this when I left home to travel the world and saw poverty, neglect and extreme living conditions in third-world countries, which fortunately was not something I'd experienced growing up.

You may have seen colleagues getting promotions above you, even though you put in the same amount of effort and work. This could be because of bias – conscious or unconscious – against your cultural background, gender, age, ethnicity or marital status. If this were to happen again and you noticed it, would you say something? What if the situation were reversed? This is the question an upstander leader needs to think about: 'Will I actively protect equality in my workplace even if the inequality is benefiting me?'

The UK's *Equality Act 2010* legally requires workplaces to proactively promote equality in their activities and decisions. The Act lists nine characteristics that are protected: age, disability, gender reassignment, marriage and civil partnership, pregnancy and maternity, race, religion or belief, sex, and sexual orientation. The list's breadth should mean that there is little problem with equality in the workplace, though this isn't what we see in reality. Other jurisdictions have similar acts, and I encourage you to explore the relevant legislation for where you work.

While guidelines may be put in place to protect and support these characteristics, guidelines do not always affect culture. An equality-focused workplace culture allows workers to thrive. I remember being in a boardroom meeting with a client telling me to get the job done as I was a ticking time bomb before I started having children. This is a very prominent assumption about young career-driven women. I also had a friend call me in 2020 to ask my advice about whether she should apply for a job, or whether it would be unfair as she intended to have children in the next few years. She thought that maybe she should pass on the promotion to her male counterpart. Biases around equality do not always come from other people – they can also be internal biases that arise through social programming.

As an upstander leader, ask yourself whether you are providing fairness and equality to all your colleagues and your team so that they can do their best work, feel seen and heard, and trust your judgement. If you don't value equality and don't check your own biases, it'll impact your reputation with members of the upstander generation, who value an equal playing field. You could also limit your own success in your career if you believe you're not good enough or don't deserve a promotion because of your background, race, sexual orientation, age, gender, or whatever it may be.

Jo Farrell is the general manager of Kane Construction and founder of Build Like a Girl, and has 25 years' experience in the construction industry. In 2021 I interviewed Jo on the Jessica Hickman Podcast, and she talked about her early career within the construction industry. For many months I'd followed Jo on LinkedIn, and she'd often shared her story of struggles as a woman in a male-dominated industry. Jo told me that during her early career, she'd had to work for free for three months, as it was hard to get the door open as a woman in the construction industry. She heard comments such as, 'This is not a girl's job', and, 'We can't have girls on site'.

In Jo's words, she had to badger a male business owner to give her a chance at an apprenticeship. When this guy finally gave Jo a chance and signed her up as an apprentice, she had to struggle and fight to prove her worth. Not only did she have to work for free for three whole months, she also had to show that she was equally as strong and confident as her male counterparts. Jo said the guy made it as difficult as possible.

One day, Jo was handed a shovel and told to dig a hole. When Jo asked, 'How deep?' she was told not to ask any questions. She told me that she ended up digging a hole almost as deep as she was tall, and she was then directed to fill the hole in again – so it was a pointless task after all. Once Jo had dug and filled the hole, she was told to dig another. The aim was to demoralise her, but Jo just got on with it.

This was not all that she experienced as a woman in the construction industry. On another occasion, she was locked in a portable toilet, which was then pushed over with her inside. Many other women in construction have experienced similar mistreatment. Jo told me the aim was to break her down and prove that she did not belong in the industry.

Jo talked about how there are often no female bathrooms on job sites, which can lead to unsafe environments and a lack of privacy for women. There is a gaslighting mentality within the construction industry, where people use toxic language such as, 'Everyone in this day and age is too politically correct'. Jo was accused of being unable to take a joke. She told me, 'It's the exclusion – you know it's wrong, and if you call it out, it can compound'. People can then turn their back on you, and work becomes a lonely place.

By sharing this, Jo emphasises that being an upstander is not always easy – it takes courage. As a leader, it's important that you support the courageous humans who speak up and seek support.

Jo founded her business to inspire other young women. Build Like a Girl develops female apprentices and mentors, and encourages women to step into the construction industry and into their true power. When I spoke to Jo on my podcast, she shared many tips, and my favourite is to get a strong mentor – someone who believes in you and who you can go to when you feel like you need someone to chat to.

Why is it important to provide equality in your workplace? Well, how would you feel if someone dear to you were treated like Jo was? Are you providing a mentoring and coaching culture in your workplace?

*

In this chapter, we've discussed the importance of empathy, ethics and equality at work and in your leadership. These are the perfect conditions in which to establish an upstander culture.

As a leader, it is important you understand the three Es, as they are fundamental to your success in this decade of disruption and beyond. Look around your workplace. Are empathy, ethics and equality present? What do you see?

PART III

THE FIVE STEPS TO BECOMING AN UPSTANDER

Taking your place as an upstander is about embracing the five critical steps: Look, Listen, Learn, Lead and Love. Let's look at each step in turn.

Chapter 7

Look

This chapter explores awareness. It covers how to scan your current environment to become a more observant leader, be aware of what's going on in your environment, recognise the archetypes and zones, and look at areas of your life where you may have become a passive bystander.

Upstander leaders fine-tune their observation skills and look at the relationships within their teams. Are you conscious of the relationship dynamics and red flags in your team and workplace? We can lose sight of this when we get too caught up in the business or become complacent. We all have blind spots, just like when driving a car.

Leaders' blind spots need attention. Leaders are super busy – they tell me that there is never-ending work to do juggling tasks and relationships. As a leader, you might feel like you're on a hamster wheel, constantly chasing your tail with an ever-increasing to-do list. The busier you are, the more likely it is that you'll fail to see what is happening right under your nose within your team, or to see how you come across as a leader. In this chapter, I will show you how to look effectively and quickly.

Looking helps to move you out of the Unconscious, Avoidance and Uncomfortable Zones that we discussed in chapter 5. By actively focusing on your observation skills, you can become a better leader and have more self-awareness.

When I experienced bullying, I got caught in the whirlwind, and my judgement as a leader was clouded. I spent long days and nights in fear mode, and often I failed to notice what was happening around me. I remember looking in the mirror one morning and not recognising the woman before me. I had failed to observe my declining weight, the black bags under my eyes, the sadness in my eyes and the frown lines across my forehead. I was caught up in surviving.

I also failed to observe some of the relationship dynamics forming around me. I remember vividly deciding to be alert – to watch how my bully treated me compared to others, and how others would respond to his presence. My observations gave me a crash course in good, bad and ugly leadership. Leaders were running around unconscious, avoidant and often uncomfortable.

I observed who would support me and who wouldn't support me. One day, a colleague pulled me aside and said, 'I have observed what is happening here and it's not okay. You do not deserve this treatment'. Hearing this led to a breakthrough for me in understanding that I was not making up the bullying in my mind, and also confirmed that people were turning a blind eye. Upon scanning the environment and reflecting on the whole experience, I realised most of my colleagues were aware of the situation and sat in the Uncomfortable Zone, while the leadership teams were in the Avoidance Zone.

I learned to observe my bully from a third-party perspective, which is a fundamental skill that has helped me and many of my clients thrive. Observing a situation from a third-party viewpoint allows you to more clearly understand the other person's behaviour and motives, and helps you document it. Often, challenging situations can become emotionally charged, which can cloud thinking, decision-making and leadership.

When you are being bullied, the bullying consumes all aspects of your life. When you are triggered, your emotions blow your judgement out of proportion, which can cause you to act irrationally – retaliating or, in my case, melting down in tears in the workplace. This was exactly what my bully had in mind, and it allowed him to gain the power and control he desired. Objective observation allows you to analyse the circumstances and determine whether you are being bullied, and whether it's causing harm to you as a leader or to your workplace culture.

Proactive observation – what am I not seeing?

When you practise proactive observation, you can see examples of upstander and bystander behaviours that are invisible to others. Proactive observation means observing something or someone in order to gain information. You are looking to find the overall dynamics of the workplace and whether it is psychologically safe for your employees. Specifically, look for the energy (or lack thereof) in the room, as well the communication, conversation dynamics and level of connection between employees – this should give you a sense of whether your workplace is fostering upstanders. A true leader should observe, value others and be constantly mindful of the emotional environment they're fostering in their workplace. A workplace leader is either part of the problem or part of the solution.

In 1992, Massachusetts Institute of Technology researchers Arien Mack and Irvin Rock coined the term 'inattentional blindness' to describe the failure to notice a visible but unexpected object because attention is engaged on another task, event or object. It happens to all of us. Seeing is often assumed to be a conscious process, but the truth is that it is largely unconscious. Our senses are bombarded with so much information – sights, sounds, smells, and so on – that our minds can't process it all at once.

It's important for us to be observant at work so that we can notice toxic behaviours. We cannot fix what we cannot see. If we fail to observe our surroundings, we risk falling into the bystander effect, and our leadership suffers.

Bystanders in the Unconscious Zone are often walking around oblivious to the issues that everyone else sees. A lot can be learned through observation. For example, through thousands of hours of delivering workshops, I have developed the skill of scanning the room and observing people's comfort level, fatigue, hidden agendas and even emotional turmoil. I can read these because I have been practising paying attention to them over a long period of time.

Do you use the power of observation to succeed at work? A client and I were discussing how to develop his leadership at work. He told me he watched the high-flying leaders and observed what they did, and showed me a journal of notes he had collected over the months we'd been working together. He told me he had used the power of observation to observe the leaders' self-awareness, how they managed and dealt with conflict, and how they opted to be an upstander in certain meetings and situations.

He observed that if you work with a person who has power over you, you can learn how they act – their flaws, their weaknesses and their leadership quirks. You can observe the way they carry themselves, their clothing, their outward image, the words they speak, how they get what they want, and how they define success. You can look at what results they get from interacting with others. Observation is a powerful tool for learning from your current leadership.

Take a look around your workplace. Do employees look happy and productive? Who looks like they're struggling? What about them tells you that? Do staff look excited and proud to work there, or do they look fearful and stressed? What about body language? Are people slumped or curled up?

Self-awareness – looking at your inner world

Equally important as scanning other people is taking a deep dive into your inner world. Diving into your own emotional, physical and mental state means that you can regulate yourself. If you're aware of these things, you'll be able to recognise when your own actions bother or anger someone else. Self-awareness means being mentally and emotionally present – ideally all the time, but that's a high bar to set. Self-awareness means catching yourself and quickly returning to a state of clarity and calmness. This is a crucial part of being an upstander leader.

Self-awareness means exploring whether you are a problem or a solution. It means asking yourself, 'Am I acting as an upstander or a bystander?' At times, neglecting my own inner wellbeing meant I failed to observe how my emotions were impacting others. For example, when I experienced bullying, my home life was affected. Looking back, I wasn't able to regulate myself, which then impacted the people I loved.

This does not extend to mental illness or breakdowns. This is about our day-to-day blind spots. Please seek specialist medical help if your observations suggest that you need it. For example, sleepless nights, drinking alcohol excessively, feeling low for long periods of time and chronic fatigue are all signs that you need to seek advice from a specialist, or contact your GP or psychologist.

In my case, when I was in the same room as my bully, I was self-aware enough to know that I needed to avoid being in his personal space when possible. I would dodge him like a bullet, but I was constantly in fight-flight-or-freeze mode, which impacted my health. In the end, this hyper-awareness and consistently heightened nervous system led to me being hospitalised. I didn't have the self-awareness to realise how the situation was impacting me on a physical, mental, and emotional level until the burnout and overwhelm consumed me.

By becoming more self-aware and subsequently recognising their strengths, weaknesses and hidden biases, leaders gain the trust of their team members, increase their own credibility and lead by example.

The first step to self-awareness is to look at past issues you've had with people and be honest with yourself. Something that helped me is journaling my experience – writing it down as if I were a third-party observer, and noting the emotions and reactions.

Sometimes it's hard to think that we might have messed up. Don't beat yourself up over the actions that prolong or cause a negative environment. I have learned that it is beneficial to journal not only emotion but also factual information, as this can help you later if a situation escalates out of control – you may need to make a report and use your documented evidence.

Environment – what am I ignoring?

It's not just the people in your work environment and their psychological safety that you need to look at, but also the work environment itself.

Plants and animals are adapted to live in a specific environment. They need certain temperatures to survive. Plants need the right amount of rain and sunlight. Plants and animals can't put on a sweater if it's too cold, and they can't go into an air-conditioned building if it's too hot. They depend on the environment to be just right for them.

Often, people end up in an environment that is determined by their job; for example, a construction worker on a development site, or a miner underground, or a lawyer in a big inner-city building. However, post-pandemic, many people working from home have been able to control their environment and have worked out what is best for them.

As a leader, when you observe the work environment, you are looking for not only physical safety risks (which we will come to in a moment) but also whether the environment is:

· dingy or light
· messy or organised
· uncomfortable or comfortable
· unsafe or safe (or ergonomic)
· risky or structured
· institutional or homely
· noisy or quiet
· crowded or spacious
· outdated or modern.

These factors, when taken into account, can all add up to a relaxed and safe environment in which people can do their best work and be productive, creative and innovative.

Now let's consider physical safety. In many industries, employees face high risks. Safety hazards could include forklift drivers going too fast or not observing their blind spots, an office employee leaving a bag on a floor, or someone running a power cord across a walking zone. Mistakes, errors and accidents on the job can be disastrous, causing injury or even loss of life, but can also be costly in materials and time wasted, decreasing top-line profits. When it comes to safety, we need to follow legislation requirements.

It's in the leader's best interest for employees to be mindful of mistakes and take interest in what is going on around them. Despite precautionary measures, things can easily be missed. Training and engaging employees to look for risks can help them realise the importance of the role they play in maintaining a safe workplace environment. Having vigilant and alert employees looking out for danger helps you become a proactive leader. The role of observer needs to sit with every employee, not just the leadership team.

It's important to create an observant environment; I know first-hand how detrimental a toxic environment can be to success. Many books I've read over the years have claimed that you become a product of your environment. I was at a Tony Robbins conference in Sydney in September 2017, Australia, where he stated that you become the five people you spend the most time with. As an example, I used to work with someone who constantly moaned about the weather. Over time, I started to repeat the negative pattern of waking up and feeling deflated if it was raining or cold. I've also worked with people who would gossip and talk about other people in the lunchroom; looking back, I was sucked into that energy and wasn't observant about how toxic that could be.

There's a thing called mirroring, where humans copy each other. For example, when one person yawns, another person can catch on, and it can be contagious. I experience another example of mirroring when I hang out with my best friend, Tiffany. Tiffany is notorious for having giggling fits. When I see Tiffany fall into one of her giggling fits, I find myself being pulled into the vortex and mirroring her behaviour. I also notice that, when I hang out with certain friends, I adapt my style of communication to meet theirs.

During a coaching session I ran, the team highlighted that the previous office environment had made them feel claustrophobic and unmotivated, and lowered their mood. Basic changes were made to the environment – they put a lick of white paint over the dark and dingy walls, they introduced a few plants, and they also did a team development day at which they produced a piece of artwork that they could put up on the wall. All low-budget stuff, but effective.

In 2018, I went on a business trip and found myself in the head office of Hootsuite in Canada. The office was decked out in the style of a cool ski lodge, smack-bang in the city centre of Vancouver. Staff could bring their dogs to work, and people would dress cool and relaxed.

If you want to create a safe, productive environment, talk to your employees and see how they feel in the environment. It doesn't have to be a big costly office fit-out with funky sofas and chill-out meditation zones – low-budget changes can have a positive impact, such as painting the walls, adding some plants and creating breakout spaces for innovation and change. You don't need a fancy external environment to create a community of trust; you just have to observe and understand what people want and care about. If you're not sure, simply ask them.

Exercise: Environment check

Look at your environment. Does it energise you or make you feel lethargic? Visualise a place in your imagination that makes you feel grounded, calm, and focused. Look at other workplaces that have won awards for creating a great environment to work in. How could you incorporate some of these ideas?

Red flags – what am I tolerating?

Now we'll look at how easy it is to observe a problem but still ignore it. Some issues can feel too hard to tackle. This might be because we are used to them, we fear alternatives (such as walking away), we are too busy and distracted, we believe we don't deserve better, or people normalise them. I have friends who become so focused on being in a relationship or having job success that they choose to ignore red flags in their crumbling relationships or careers. I've done this myself. Life is not meant to be lived by focusing only on one aspect at a time – you need balance in all areas, from work to family, friends and personal enjoyment of life.

Red flags indicate situations that will become emergencies if you don't stop and attend to them. While the other forms of observation we've covered are about making gradual changes over time, noticing red flags is essential for risk mitigation. Red flags can be so blatant that they almost punch us in the face, but a busy mind can easily miss them. When we pause and reflect, or someone draws them to our attention, we can kick ourselves for missing them and risking getting hurt or hurting others.

I have a running joke with some friends that they run at red flags like bulls. To be honest, I have ignored some pretty huge red flags in my own work and business. A few years back, I did a consultancy gig that was a real eye-opener. I thought it would be a good opportunity to look at how the company owner did business, modelled behaviour and became a mentor, and see how success played out. However, what I observed was how not to do business. I had a gut feeling about six months in that something was a little fishy, but I believed the intentions of the social impact were good enough that maybe the leadership just needed a face lift. I ended up spending 12 months of my time working in partnership with a person who spun a web of lies to himself, his peers and his investors, which ultimately left a bad taste in the mouths of the clients, the employees and myself.

The whole experience caused me to become anxious, uncomfortable and, over time, avoidant. I also observed my own mental health, trust and confidence diminish. Over time, my brand-new business started to take off, which led to negative comments and a little jealousy from this person. We parted ways in the end when an invoice didn't get paid and things got a little sour. I felt disappointed, and even more so when I found out the true extent of the falsehood, manipulations and false promises.

I am now proactive at noticing red flags in both my professional and personal life and calling them out. Before I agree to anything with a person, I investigate whether our values are aligned and check whether the individual has the three Es – empathy, ethics and equality – as core principles. I use my own self-awareness to dial into my gut instincts. Is this opportunity going to benefit me? Does it feel right internally? What could be the potential red flags I'm missing?

To spot a red flag, you need all three elements in this chapter – proactive observation, or looking for what is not obvious at first glance; self-awareness, or observing your own thoughts and feelings; and awareness of environment – is something unsafe, or just unfriendly or uncomfortable?

*

Stop being blind to problems in others, yourself and your environment. Stop creating blind spots to ignore red flags. Move out of the Unconscious, Avoidance and Uncomfortable Zones, and observe your inner and outer environments.

Chapter 8

Listen

As a leadership coach, a common problem I hear is that communication needs to improve. 'Communication' is a broad umbrella, covering public, private, collective and interpersonal communication. Digging deeper with my clients over the last three years, I've noticed a common pattern: the root of the issue is people's poor listening skills. Leaders who struggle to proactively communicate with their employees may find that their poor listening skills and inability to show empathy cause significant problems in their approach to teamwork and leadership.

The bystander mentality is prominent in many organisations, and leaders are often not only blind to what's happening but also deaf, often selectively. Listening means picking up on not only the words and ideas your colleagues are contributing, but the subtle clues to what lies beneath the surface in body language, inflection and team dynamics. As a leader, are you an empty vessel who is positively listening for opportunities? Being an empty vessel is about creating space and emptying your tank of questions, thoughts and the busyness from your day in order to truly listen. It's about minimising internal dialogue and holding space for your intuition to do its best work.

Listening is an underappreciated form of leadership mastery. Step two of becoming an upstander leader is to become an active listener.

The greatest gift that you can give to another person is your full attention. Leaders who develop their listening skills have better relationships and earn the respect of their team, clients and peers.

When I first started working in the Top End of Australia, hearing the suicide and mental health statistics was alarming. I couldn't believe what I heard. It was an eye-opening crash course in how serious men's mental health was, particularly in the fly-in fly-out industry. After my first induction, I lay in bed replaying the stats over and over in my head. I wondered how, as a people leader, I could make sure that employees felt seen, heard and valued at my workplace. I also wondered how I could develop enough trust for people to feel that they could talk to me and I would truly listen to them.

Therefore, the listening tour was born. Every day I would head out from my portacabin office and walk around the large oil and gas project, building rapport with the workforce – asking curious questions about their families and hobbies, and finding out why they chose to come and work on the project and live in camps away from family and friends.

Often I would hear, 'We come to work to have a good quality of life outside of work. We earn good money to put our kids through school, or to have a nice house'. There was always a motivation for choosing to work long hours away from home on some of the most remote projects across Australia. The power of my listening skills enabled me to develop deep relationships and trust.

Over time, we developed a leadership listening tour. I would encourage the leadership team to schedule time in their calendars each week on a rotating basis. I initially went with them to the job front with the simple aim of listening and learning about our colleagues, employees and peers. If I found the conversation was naturally swaying towards productivity or safety, I would nudge the senior leader to remind them that this was a rapport-building listening tour.

The team on each job front would see us come in well in advance. We would wave icy poles and water bottles. In Darwin, these were always a welcome sight. At first, the workforce was apprehensive. They assumed the leaders were coming to spy on them or berate them about safety. They would ask, 'What do they really want? Are there hidden agendas and motivations?' However, over time, with the consistent effort of showing up and actively listening from a place of empathy and with no agenda, the workers began to trust me and share their experiences of deep-rooted issues such as mental health, illnesses, suicidal thoughts, and sex and drug addiction.

I even had workmates call me to say, for example, 'Joey is at the camp, intoxicated from last night. We told him to stay in his room and not risk failing the drug and alcohol test'. This was a culture of trust where they felt that they could call and be supported, not judged. After all, I would rather they call and be honest than come to work and potentially risk their life or the lives of others.

There was a change in culture. The power of simply listening opens up a blank canvas, which can then be filled with shared knowledge that could potentially save a life. Conscious listening becomes a base for trust.

Here's a truth bomb, though: it wasn't quite the same for all of the leadership team. Some continued to put their egos and agendas ahead of listening and never bridged the gap of trust.

An upstander leader is adept at consciously listening, asking great questions, and listening to their own body and intuition. But how do you get there?

The power of conscious listening

You probably listen in on conversations and meetings every day, but only at a surface level, and you incorporate your own agendas into that listening. Therefore, you rarely receive an accurate portrayal of what's actually being said. This is common.

What does it mean to practise conscious listening? When you listen to someone with this intention, you're letting them know, 'I am interested. I care and I seek to understand what you are saying. I am not judging you, and I acknowledge how you feel about this issue'. I will explain some listening techniques later in this chapter.

Are you a conscious and empathetic listener? Do you provide welcome validation to the speaker? I've mentioned the concept of the empty vessel. I started to practise becoming an empty vessel when I was doing my coaching certificate. Previously, I would bounce between coaching clients with my mind full of my to-do list. Now, before I sit down and engage with anyone in a coaching session, I imagine myself visually emptying all of the chitter-chatter out of my mind and creating an empty space, so that person has me truly and consciously listening.

Conscious listening improves mutual understanding and builds trust. It takes time and patience, but it is a skill that can be acquired and developed with practice. It does require effort. It requires full concentration to hear not just the words being said but the nuances, the undertones and the subtext. It involves listening with all senses and looking for both verbal and non-verbal messages – maintaining eye contact, smiling, noticing frowns, and generally gauging how the other person is feeling by their facial expressions.

Through conscious listening – and using body language, such as nodding as feedback – you can encourage the speaker and make them feel more at ease. This sense of engagement helps build rapport, encouraging more open communication. When a colleague comes to you and discloses a problem or even toxic behaviours happening at work, upstander leaders and conscious listeners should remain neutral and non-judgmental. Try not to take sides or form opinions, especially early in the conversation.

Conscious listening is about patience. Pauses are okay and can be a very useful tactic. Listeners should not be tempted to jump in with questions too early on, or comment every time there are a few seconds of silence. Conscious listening involves giving the other person time to explore their thoughts and feelings. Give the speaker your full attention, removing distractions, noticing your thoughts and directing your attention to what the speaker is saying, and pause with tact. A helpful tactic for practising conscious listening, especially in meetings, is to put phones away. Otherwise, you'll often see people checking their phones; it's one of my pet peeves.

Conscious listening is a choice to pay full attention, which people notice, and which means that you stay fully informed and connected. If you don't do this, you could miss a piece of valuable information that later turns out to be a source of problems. Also, you can miss connecting with another person and be perceived as rude, neglectful and a poor leader. Conscious listening is an essential skill to build to become an upstander leader and develop your upstander culture.

Having worked in various places, including rehabilitation centres and homeless projects, I've spent a lot of time training myself to be a conscious listener. In the middle of the COVID-19 pandemic, all of my business went online, and I needed to not only fill my human connection cup but serve the community during one of the toughest periods I have seen in my lifetime; so, in 2020, I started doing some frontline work at a youth homeless project in Sydney. Having previously volunteered in many homeless projects back in the UK, I knew I had to open my heart, practise empathy and, most of all, create space for conscious listening in order to connect with the youths living in the project.

The shelter was used to place youth in emergency accommodation and was full. On my first shift, a 16-year-old approached me in the office. They pulled their hood up, and when I said, 'Hello', they stayed silent. I introduced myself, and they stayed silent. A bit uncomfortable, I attempted a few questions. 'Are you hungry? Do you like this show on TV? Are you okay with me chatting to you?' Silence. The questions got some shrugs, and the body language was very closed off and avoidant.

During my next shift, the same person came to my office and slumped down on the couch next to the office desk. They removed their hood, smiled and introduced themselves. For an hour, the person chatted, giggled, talked and then eventually said, 'I've had enough now', and skipped off back to their room.

What I came to learn about this person was that they suffered from various mental health illnesses, which left them experiencing different moods. On days when I observed open body language, I would sit back, listen, ask questions and consciously hold space for the person. I would listen to every word, nodding and smiling. On the days when they were low, I would practise silence and hold space for them. Over time, a rapport was built. Even on the low days, the person would tell me how they felt and what their thoughts were. I would respond with a few words and questions, such as, 'Do you feel safe? Can I please check on you this evening?'

I wanted to tell you this story because during a debrief, one of my colleagues mentioned that the silence – waiting for questions to be answered and consciously listening – made them feel uncomfortable. They said that they often have to ask questions to fill the silence. This made me think about the art of conscious listening and how it's not a natural default.

Silence does not mean that the individual does not understand, but rather that they are listening and thinking, and may wait to hear others' ideas before expressing their own views. There are times when Indigenous Australians may remain non-committal or may be awaiting community support or input. Allow for periods of silence in interviews, meetings and general conversation for these reasons.

Here are some great ways to build your conscious listening skills so that you can hear what the other person is truly saying (and not find the awkward silences quite so awkward):

- Focus your attention squarely on the other person.
- Listen to their answers and tap into their feelings.
- Look for clues in gestures and body language, such as shrugging, blinking and hunching.
- Notice the other person's energy, mood, tone and voice, looking for emotional cues.
- Paraphrase what you hear and clarify whether you understand. This is a powerful tool I use in coaching.
- Listen and look for the impact of what you have said to the person. Is it bringing about a higher or lower energy? Are they leaning in or withdrawing?
- Listen for what isn't being said – for example, they don't mention being upset when they look upset.

What to be mindful of

It's easy to assume listening is a basic skill, but there are many intruder forms of listening that can come from our own agendas. For example:

- Interrupting – speaking over someone in a meeting and jumping the gun, dismissing the feelings of others and feeling that your point is more relevant
- Finishing other people's sentences, as if you're a mind reader
- Rehearsing a response in your head before the person speaking has even finished
- Simply hearing the words but not deeply and consciously listening because you are distracted, which risks only receiving half of the information being conveyed

- Being culturally appropriate – for example, for many non-Indigenous people eye contact is considered a key component of communication, but some Indigenous people consider it rude or disrespectful to look someone straight in the eye. It's important to be aware of cultural context and to upskill in the area of cross-culture communication.

An upstander leader who practises the art of conscious listening puts their ego aside and holds space for the other person.

Exercise: Explore your habits

Explore some of the habits you might have formed from the list above, then think about what habits need to be learned or unlearned. The listening styles described in that list are not helpful, and could potentially hinder you as a leader and undermine the creation of an upstander culture.

Busy leaders listen less – true or false? A director I coach told me that she's often too busy – she hears sound, but no words register. I found this fascinating, and we began to unpack it. She said she has a glass office, and members of her team come in constantly to drop information on her verbally like bombs, often when she is writing or reviewing important documents. Upon conducting a 360-degree review, her staff responded that they believed she was often too busy to listen to them.

Reflecting on this, we established that she did not have the capacity to listen for a full eight hours a day, and she had big tasks to focus on. She needed to carve out a dedicated time to consciously listen and be present for her people.

This made me reflect on times when I have been simply hearing words but not consciously listening. For example, when my husband comes home from work, I have been guilty of being buried deep in a task (such as writing this book) and, when he comes in to tell me a story about his day or attempts to connect, I nod and smile and continue my task. One day he pulled me up on this and asked, 'What did I just say?' I was caught red-handed. It wasn't that I don't love him, respect him and absolutely want to hear about his day, but I was caught up in my own busyness and not consciously creating space to truly listen and connect. I realised this was a missed opportunity in our relationship, so I make a conscious effort now to connect when he gets home from work. Also, no phones at the dinner table.

Strong leaders serve the people closer to the frontline. They challenge the status quo. They walk the talk and consciously listen.

Exercise: How do you practise listening?

Reflect on how you practise listening as a leader. Do you listen more at home or at work, or do both need a little bit more attention? Create space in your day. Manage your calendar and stop booking yourself out for the entire day. Can someone on your team be part of that meeting instead of you? Does it need to go for an hour, or would 30 minutes suffice? Give yourself time for reflection and space throughout the day, so that when you are talking with someone, you can give them your full attention and practise your conscious listening.

Ask open-ended questions

Peter Drucker has been quoted as stating, 'The more serious mistakes are not being made as a result of wrong answers. The truly dangerous thing is asking the wrong question'. People view leaders as having the answers, but actually leaders should be asking the right questions and eliciting answers from their people – especially the frontline workers, who are the eyes and ears of the business. You need to be better at doing this, and your organisations need to encourage and enable people to give answers.

Like listening, asking great questions is a skill. Powerful questions are oriented towards the future – they question opportunities and goals. Rather than being problem-orientated and focused on the 'what', future-focused questions keep us moving forward and force us to expand our ideas. Future-focused questions are more often open-ended than closed-ended. Open-ended questions do not have a single-word answer; answers can be as long and as expansive as the speaker wants them to be.

Open-ended questions are great for extracting information – for example, 'What is your favourite part of working for this company?' Closed-ended questions have binary answers ('Yes' or 'No') and are great for decision and precision – for example, 'Do you like working here?' They go together like salt and pepper. Both are widely underestimated as leadership tools; both take practice.

Open-ended questions are a powerful tool for eliciting information from the people on the ground and discovering your bystander blind spots. Asking great questions helps you move away from a typical hierarchy of information directed downwards and towards a two-way flow of feedback. It also allows you to find out what your people's needs are and avoid top-heavy decisions.

When running workshops, I actively listen to participants' stories and enjoy encouraging more information by asking open-ended questions. Then, as I move through the workshop, I refer back to the participants' stories. This not only builds rapport but gives credit to the story or idea presented, and also allows the participants to see that I consciously listen to their stories and find them valuable. Participants have reported feeling seen, heard and valued for sharing or articulating a point. All people want to be seen, observed, cared about, listened to, valued, loved and respected.

Darwin typically has two seasons – hot and dry, and wet and humid. Wet season is a hard slog for many in the workforce. The Territorians refer to it as the onset of 'mango madness' – the heat and humidity are known to send you a little crazy. On one wet Wednesday during my time there, one of the supervisors contacted me on the radio and asked me to come out to the job front immediately. Jumping in the ute, I travelled across the site. As I looked out at the blue wharf and the crystal-clear water, it blew me away yet again how beautiful the Top End is. Shame you can't swim because of the crocs, but that's another story.

One of the workers – for the sake of confidentiality, I'll call him TJ – was slumped over on one of the large toolboxes. His supervisor waved me over and pulled me aside, saying that TJ was not in a good headspace. He had asked to chat with me. I knew TJ fairly well. He was one of the loudest, most confident jokers on site – extremely energetic, charismatic and fun. Today, he looked like shit. His eyes had dark rings around them. He looked almost green, and tired – oh so very tired.

'Hey mate, how're you going?' I said. TJ looked up at me vacantly and replied, 'Not good, Jess. Not good'. Reading the cue, I realised that TJ probably wasn't feeling comfortable in his current position on site. I said, 'Let's get you in the car, buddy. We'll go get a coffee and you can grab a clean shirt'. TJ was wet from the Darwin sweat and humidity. Jumping in the car, I remember looking across at him and seeing his vacant look out of the window as I manoeuvred out of the car spot.

During the drive back, he closed his eyes, and I could feel that it was not the moment to overload him with questions. Once back, we set up in the medical room – I made TJ a coffee and he slumped back on the plastic chair. I just sat in silence next to him, sipping my coffee and looking out of the window, mirroring his body language. After a couple of minutes of silence, TJ said, 'I'm not in a good place, Jess'. Looking across at him, I leaned on the table and held my ear, signalling I was listening. TJ then told me his marriage was over. He was not sleeping. He felt depressed. He was drinking a lot each day, and he was contemplating making some life decisions that he might regret later.

I moved my chair to face TJ after asking permission to do so. I leaned in and consciously listened to every word he told me over the next two hours, nodding and showing concern on my face. Once TJ slumped back and paused for a while, I found it was the perfect time to ask the right questions.

Paraphrasing what TJ had told me, I asked questions around safety that I'd learned in my mental health training:

- Are you safe to go back to camp?
- Are you at risk of hurting yourself or others?
- Can I support you to call your doctor or mental health practitioner?
- Can you tell me more about X, Y and Z?
- How are you feeling now?

Using a mixture of open and closed questions allowed TJ to expand further on how he was feeling, and together we made a mental health care plan to get him safely back to the camp and to see his doctor, a mental health practitioner. TJ agreed to the support and thanked me for listening. He said he had not told anyone about his situation as he was ashamed. I reassured TJ that I did not judge him and that the details of his story would remain confidential, but he agreed that I could brief the mental health practitioner on his symptoms so he could get an emergency appointment and the support he needed.

TJ returned to work a few weeks later, bright-eyed and bubbly. His charismatic self was back. He pulled me aside and thanked me again for listening. He made a request to share his mental health journey with his colleagues and peers. He asked that I help him prepare a speech, which he wanted to share during the toolbox talk (a regular, informal talk that is a powerful safety tool for construction and industrial companies). TJ said:

'Never bottle it up, lads. Find someone you trust that will listen non-judgmentally and never feel you are alone. I felt I was alone for too long, and just having someone to listen and share my truth with was the step I needed to get the support I desperately needed. I will be that person for you. If you ever feel alone, I promise I will consciously listen and point you in the right direction.'

He shared some personal stories, and I could see a twinkle of a tear in the big, burly scaffolders' eyes. One of the scaffolders stood up at the end and thanked TJ for his bravery, his vulnerability and sharing his story. He said, 'What's interesting about your story, TJ, is you are always the fun, bubbly one, but I've realised that mental health has no face. Let's all commit to listening, asking great questions and speaking up when we need help'.

Ask open-ended questions to facilitate individual insights and allow others to elaborate. Think about open questions in this way: you want to focus on the 'what' and the 'how', and avoid the 'why'. Some questions to get more information – what, when, where – may be necessary. The best questions, 'what' and 'how', encourage expansive thinking. Use information-gathering questions – who, when, where – sparingly, but as needed. Ask questions that show you care and want clarification about what they're saying: 'I'd like to understand your view on this situation. Your feedback is valued'.

It's important to ask questions in an exploratory way; for example, 'I've noticed that you've been running late more often recently, and I was wondering if everything is okay?' Check your understanding by restating what they have said. Summarise the facts and feelings. I use statements such as, 'So what I am hearing is...' or, 'Correct me if I am wrong or miss something...'

Avoid 'why' questions, as they can often sound judgmental and put people into defence mode, even if that's not your intention. Try rephrasing 'why' questions to begin with 'what' or 'how' – for example, 'What factors did you consider?' or 'How did you decide what to do?' Avoid using questions to hide advice – for example, 'Do you think X, Y, Z could work?' Avoid embarrassing the person by saying things like, 'Everyone is noticing...'

Once you have mastered the art of asking great questions, practise the art of silence. To be honest, I had to master the art of silence while studying for my coaching qualification and mental health certificate. Silence can be uncomfortable for a lot of people, but in my experience it creates an opportunity for those reflective thinkers and natural introverts to structure a response to open questions.

I also recommend that everyone undertake some form of mental health response training, such as Mental Health First Aid™.

Exercise: Asking the right questions

Identify 10 open, powerful, impactful questions that you could ask in your workplace and team.

Listen to your body

It would be unfair of me to finish this chapter without highlighting the importance of listening to your inner world. As leaders, we can often have moments of doubt or uncertainty. Being a leader can be very stressful. It is possible to be confident most of the time but still have moments when you question yourself. We all have an inner critic, or what I call 'the bitch in the attic'. It works hard to keep us on our toes. Leaders at the top of their game are highly aware of that internal monologue and take regular action to manage it to help them create the positive outcomes they want.

Often we attempt to manage our mind with our mind – for example, replacing a negative thought with a positive one. However, I learned the hard way that our physiology influences how we think. This is noticeable in extreme situations, when we listen to our body before anything else. For example, when I perceive myself to be in danger – such as if I hear a sound in the bushes at my farm, which could be a snake, yikes! – my body tightens up and my breathing becomes shallow. This was a state that I stayed in for three and a half years with the bullying I faced. It's often known as the fight-flight-or-freeze response.

What most people miss is that our bodies are always communicating with us, not just in emergency situations, and we must listen to them. Our bodies hold so much wisdom that we often ignore. For example, I often feel a burning in my chest and throat, which I know is stress-related. When I ask myself, 'What is triggering this?' – perhaps something important I've forgotten to do, or something coming up that I'm nervous about – I can take action to respond to my body.

Our bodies often know things before our minds do. The gut has even been described as a 'second brain'. It's important to understand this as a leader. If your body's messages are not managed correctly, this is when burnout can happen. I know firsthand the damaging effects of ignoring your body's signals. During my bullying experience, I had a lot of symptoms that I didn't understand at the time – I couldn't connect the dots. I had repetitive strain injury, aches and pains, and tightness in my arms, legs and neck. My stomach was constantly tight, which impacted my gut health. I would break out in rashes. My eyes would swell. My throat would become dry and tight. My chest would often feel like there was an elephant standing on it.

Here's a leadership context in which you could apply this. Say you're in a meeting and start feeling a bit unusual – hot and sweaty, with a wheezy feeling in your stomach. This could be your intuition telling you that your recent decision was wrong, there's an angle that hasn't been considered, or the approach you're discussing may not be right. Maybe you suspect that you're missing some key information or facts. In my case, if I notice that the intentions of others are malicious, I feel this in my gut, and my body has been tuned to notice risks. If I ignore this feeling and don't listen to my body signals, this can lead to sleepless nights. I can wake at night with the same feeling that I have messed up some decisions or missed some opportunities.

Consider this a way of connecting to a part of you that's wiser than your mind alone. You often hear leaders talk about having gut intuition or a sixth sense. The next time you get a physical sign that something is up, stop, pause and reflect. Listen to what your body is telling you. It's important to notice discomfort, as it can be helpful. Rather than running away from it, tap into it. Intuition is helpful in business. It can help you make decisions that are ethically right for you.

When was the last time you did an inventory of your physical self, of what feels good and what doesn't? As I write this passage, sitting slumped over my laptop on a rainy Saturday morning, I can instantly feel a tightness in my shoulders and in my stomach, where I hold the tension from a busy week of running workshops and running from A to B to C. My skin feels slightly dry, which reminds me to drink water. My eyes feel a little tired and heavy from a late night of writing. My muscles feel tight and sore, reminding me that yesterday was glute day at the gym.

We each have these telltale physical signs we feel worried, fatigued or run-down, or are pushing ourselves too hard. I have a ball of tension that sits right at the top of my neck. I often get ulcers on the roof of my mouth when I'm tired or run-down – 'burning the candle at both ends', as my mother would say. Some of my clients report that when they are highly stressed at work, their jaw clenches tightly and they grind their teeth at night. Panic attacks are another example – I personally experienced two panic attacks during my bullying experience, which physically floored me. As human beings, we all have symptoms when our body is telling us to slow down or that something isn't right.

Reflect on my story in chapter 2 about the car crash. Remember how I mentioned that I hadn't been feeling well all day? If only I had listened to my body. What was my intuition telling me? 'Danger, danger, danger.'

Exercise: What is your body telling you?

Take a physical inventory of your body. What are some of the signs you notice? How are you feeling? A powerful visual tool for this exercise is to draw the shape of your body and mark the spots where you have tension. Paying attention to what your body is telling you can help you be a better leader and avoid burnout.

Listen carefully when you're having a conversation, and notice how your body is feeling and responding. You can then use this awareness. One of the best ways to build trust with someone is to match their body language, breathing rate, facial expressions and vocal tone. It's almost like synchronising your emotions to theirs in real time. Try it; it's surprisingly effective and creates instant rapport. If you get a negative signal from your body – teeth grinding, heart racing, dry mouth, tight chest, muscle aches – listen to it. Perhaps halt the call or meeting and be honest with yourself.

*

The second skill that every upstander leader must learn is to listen with a full heart, body and mind, consciously creating space to listen and build rapport. For most of us, that can involve unlearning a lot of bad habits. Be ready to make some changes.

Stop simply hearing conversations or half-listening. Actively participate in conscious listening. Schedule time for listening in your diary today.

Chapter 9

Learn

The third step to becoming an upstander leader is to learn. No matter how long you've been in a leadership position, conscious and proactive learning is important. Leaders who learn have their finger on the pulse with new ways of thinking, research, statistics, and global and local big-picture trends such as the ones we explored in chapter 1. Learning about and supporting empathy, equality and ethics, and challenging your own thinking to grow and evolve to become a better people leader, will help you move from bystander to upstander.

A true upstander is constantly growing, evolving and pushing themselves outside of their comfort zone. Upstander leaders are not born – they are made. With intentional learning, you can develop into an upstander leader.

When I'm running workshops for frontline workers, especially in blue-collar industries, I often see physical and visible signs of discomfort. Being in a workshop or classroom environment is extremely uncomfortable for some people, especially if they had a negative educational experience in school, or if they have just been out of it for a long time – it can feel childish and triggering.

In 2021 I was running a mandatory workshop for a mining company, and a gentleman was extremely disgruntled about being in the room. Upon unpacking and building rapport with the man, he confessed that he thought that having to be in this workshop was bullshit. He wanted to get back to his role of being hands-on in his trade. When we chatted outside during the break, in an environment that was more comfortable, I learned that he struggled with sitting down all day. He had hated school and the classroom environment.

Learning from his story and social cues, I was able to mix up the activities. Due to it being a sunny day, I used the outdoor space to complete the team activities. The gentleman took the lead with the butcher's paper and pen and got fully into leading the group activities, laughing and joking with his peers. I was able to learn more about his role as a leader and how to support him in an environment that he found comfortable and that catered to his needs.

I'm not saying you need to change a whole structure for an individual every time, but an upstander leader is curious to learn about each individual's needs and see how they can find common ground to get the job done, while also enrolling the naysayers into their vision and mission.

To unlock your learning potential, this chapter will explore the difference between growth and fixed mindsets, learning to reject negativity, the importance of unlearning fear and judgement, and the definition of tall poppy syndrome.

Growth versus fixed mindsets

In order to understand growth and fixed mindsets, let's start with the work of an expert. According to Carol Dweck, people with a fixed mindset believe that basic qualities such as intelligence or talent are fixed as well. They spend their time documenting their intelligence or talent instead of developing it. They also believe that talent alone creates success without effort. In contrast, people with a growth mindset believe that the most basic abilities can be developed through dedication and hard work. Intelligence and talent are just the starting point.

While writing my first book, building my business and healing from workplace bullying, I had to learn to adopt a growth mindset and become a passionate learner. I was enthusiastic about learning how to turn my own adversities into my superpowers by researching and studying the impacts of bullying. That's how I learned about the bystander effect and created the concept of the upstander effect.

However, in my work I have learned that leaders often fail to become upstanders when they adopt a fixed mindset and use language such as, 'This is the way we've always done it around here', 'We can't fix what's broken', 'It will never work', 'I'm not sure this workshop or program will work', or 'Our culture is too broken'.

I witnessed both fixed-mindset and growth-mindset leaders during the COVID-19 pandemic. Some leaders I worked with used the pandemic to learn some new ways of leading, adapting and growing by:

· leaning in and navigating change
· leading remote teams for the first time
· learning how to build deeper rapport and trust with their workforce
· upskilling on new topics such as mental health awareness and future-focused leadership training.

Other leaders I worked with spent the duration of 2020 and 2021 complaining and struggling to find new ways to bounce forward into the new future of work.

The first category of leaders had a growth mindset, asking themselves how they could lead in a new way, learn and adapt to new ways of working. The second category had a fixed mindset – rigid in their approach, not open to embracing change and not curious about any new opportunities.

Even reading this book is pushing you towards a growth mindset. If you want to be an upstander leader, intentional learning is important. You need to be open to new ways of thinking and leading.

Formal school learning was never my favourite thing. I loved the environment of school and hands-on experiences, but not so much the assessment-based learning. I dreaded and hated exams. During my school years, I couldn't wait to get into the workforce – I never felt inspired to learn and go on to university. However, in later years I did. I'm the type of person who thrives on learning from my environment.

From childhood, I had the urge to understand the complexities of trauma and addiction, and how they can impact others. My biological father was an alcoholic. He did not raise me and is rarely at the forefront of my conversation. He passed away as I was approaching my twenties. Having a parent disengaged from the family is painful. Having a parent battling addiction is painful. However, despite the pain this experience brought me, it also encouraged me to grow.

At first, I felt as though I would never be able to understand my father, his behaviour and his choices, which caused me so much pain. But when I was 14, I began working and volunteering in youth settings and homeless projects across the UK. Around this time, I was given an opportunity to go on an international learning exchange to Amsterdam and studied binge drinking, drug use and sexual health. I learned that the Dutch were much more open about these topics compared to the British; and in Britain, addiction stats were higher and binge drinking was a trend. I've always been interested in learning about social impacts and issues, and I have dedicated my life to learning about topics that impact individuals, families, teams and workplaces.

I have found a passion for learning: it shapes us and our behaviours, which in turn affects our internal and external environments. For me to learn from my environment is something I enjoy and something

I wish for you. It's about adopting a growth mindset to look at adversity, and how you can become stronger following adversity.

When we are young, we are more likely to have a growth mindset. However, in the workplace, we can become fixed in our habits and beliefs. If we don't put intention into learning, we become stagnant in our thinking and fall into the bystander trap.

Exercise: Fixing fixed mindsets

Here's how to recognise fixed-mindset thinking. Watch out for thoughts or language such as the following:

- 'I just can't do that.'
- 'I'll never master that skill.'
- 'That's something only smart people can do.'
- 'That is above my pay grade.'
- 'That is something only stupid people would do.'
- 'I don't need to learn anymore – I've been in the leadership role for 10 years.'
- 'I am too busy for this workshop.'
- 'I already know how to lead.'
- 'I know what my team thinks.'

Can you think of any examples of these in your workplace or leadership?

Learning to reject negativity

To become an upstander leader, you need to address and overcome negativity, because it leads to a sense of overwhelm, team unease and toxic workplace cultures. It can be difficult to be aware how much negativity adds to your personal load until you observe how much of it you are consuming, not only in the workplace but through peer conversations, digital media and global news. While listening is important (as I explained in chapter 8), it is also vital to know when to stop listening for your own good. If your capacity to be present, observe, listen and learn is being stripped away by overconsumption of negativity, you may be putting yourself at risk of becoming a bystander. Bystanders who have not have mastered the skill of learning to reject negativity can fall into the trap of the fixed mindset.

Learn to choose what you consume and download every day. The same goes for gossip, whether it's in magazines or between teams at work. How present is gossip within your own workplace? I know that when I hear gossip about another person, it leaves me with an icky feeling in my body. To be an upstander, you need to put conscious attention into rising above gossip and being non-judgmental, rather than being an unconscious bystander – or worse, actively participating in the gossip and negativity.

When you consume too much negativity, you withdraw into bystander mode because you feel overwhelmed. This leads to toxic culture and poor leadership.

When I was a lot younger, I would get actively involved in gossip. Sometimes I would even lead the gossip. I was infatuated with celebrities and reality TV shows. On reflection, there were many times when I and my friendship group, work colleagues, peers and even family would fall into loops of negative gossip, reading the magazines and talking about individuals we'd seen on our television screens while not knowing the backstory. We would judge them based on how things played out on reality TV.

I remember a time when vicious rumours were spreading about a friend of mine. I knew they were untrue, but the gossip spiralled out of control. I also remember working at a place where someone spread a rumour that a person who was on sick leave was away because they were pregnant and the father was unknown. This turned out to be totally untrue and fabricated, which caused a lot of unease between my colleagues and, of course, really upset the person who was the subject of the gossip.

How does negativity and gossip impact your leadership? Gossip is one of the most common erosions of a healthy workplace culture. What may start out of a genuine concern for others can quickly lead to false rumours, missed information and collateral damage.

To change your culture for good and stop the spread of gossip, you need to take a proactive stance. Is there someone at work who only deals in gossip? Next time you hear them gossiping, what could you say or do to stop this behaviour? For example, if someone says, 'Sarah's behind in finishing her work, which is delaying everyone else's work', you could respond, 'What happened when you spoke to Sarah about the delays? Did you ask how the team could help and support her?' Or if office gossip is out of control and making you uncomfortable, you could say, 'I have noticed you always talk about Liam. I find this uncomfortable and don't want to be a part of these conversations'.

The importance of unlearning

Unlearning is as important as learning, especially when it comes to leadership and workplace culture. When creating an upstander culture, I often have to take leaders and their workforce on a journey of unlearning. Many people hold problematic beliefs they were pro-grammed to believe while growing up. You might have grown up in a home in which racist slurs were acceptable, or been programmed to believe certain religions were bad, toxic or dangerous. I had one leader tell me that in the household he grew up in, his dad believed women had one place, and that was at home.

Moving through this book, I hope you have recognised some bystander behaviours you need to unlearn. Upstander leaders are visionaries who look for opportunities for new stories, planning for the future with imagination and wisdom.

Unlearning is the process through which we break down the origins of our thoughts, attitudes, behaviours, feelings, habits and biases. It means stripping away the beliefs and ways of acting that have been imposed on us by our upbringing, education and society. It means challenging everything we've come to accept as the way things are supposed to be, and embracing the way things are. Most importantly, it means choosing what resonates with us and what doesn't. The power of unlearning relies on us embracing our own self-curiosity and navigating the buildings and streets of our inner world, mindfully embarking on a self-journey and deciding what stays, what goes and what needs to be renovated for us to live our authentic lives.

Once you pay attention to what needs to be unlearned, you need to replace it with new patterns of thinking to move from a fixed mindset to a growth mindset and start to see new perspectives. You no longer allow external pressure to dictate your way of life, but rather create a balance between your inner and outer worlds that develops you into a more productive leader who can build healthier, deeper relationships.

Exercise: Challenging your beliefs

Ask yourself:

- 'Where do these beliefs come from?'
- 'Is this in alignment with the life I want?'
- 'Is this consistent with my authentic self, the person I truly am?'
- 'Is this behaviour ethical?'
- 'Do I believe this to be true myself?'

These are not easy questions to ask yourself, but they are important if you want to become an upstander leader.

What has reached its expiry date in your life? What needs a spring clean? Mindsets? Relationships? What beliefs no longer serve you? What habits are holding you back from becoming the leader you want to be?

How to unlearn programmed fear

Unlearning programmed fear is something I've been focusing on. As humans, we have fear intrinsically programmed into us from birth, and it often impacts our leadership. There are three typical fear responses: fight, flight or freeze.

Fighting is an active defensive behaviour, meaning that it needs movement to occur. On the surface, the fight response can look like anger. Imagine if you saw someone lash out in a rage; it would be hard to know if their action were driven by fear or anger (or both). If your body is experiencing the fight response, your heart rate increases, you get a release of adrenaline, your pupils dilate and your muscles tighten.

Flight, or fleeing, is another active defensive behaviour. The purpose is to create space between you and the danger, which could be a predator or a workplace bully. In my workplace bullying case, this presented as running, hiding and locking myself in the bathroom.

Freezing is a passive defensive behaviour. It is an avoidance strategy that stops your motion and reduces your visibility. It can also reduce your heart rate.

Fear is also ingrained in us by others from a young age:

- 'Don't climb trees. You will hurt yourself.' This creates risk-avoidant leaders.
- 'If you haven't got something nice to say, don't say anything at all.' This leads to lost opportunities via feedback failure.
- 'Don't walk too far ahead. You might get hit by a car.' This creates fear of the future.

- 'If you don't get good grades, you will have no chance in the future.' This creates uncertainty around learning and education.
- 'If you speak up, you will be branded a troublemaker.' This creates silent bystanders.
- 'Don't ask silly questions.' This creates fear of being wrong.

Whether it's because you fear not being liked, dealing with problems head-on or creating negative outcomes, making bold decisions can be hard. But it is important – especially if that decision is to fire a bully who's tearing your team culture apart. In my work, I have learned that fear causes good leaders to become bad leaders, because they carry their fear with them as a shield of excuses. They avoid dealing with bullies, avoid speaking the truth and avoid challenging the status quo. To be an upstander leader, you need to learn what serves you and what limits you. You need to unlearn programmed fear and lean into the growth mindset of the upstander.

Becoming aware of your programmed fear is an important step in moving from bystander to upstander. I had to unlearn the fear that was programmed into me during my bullying – the self-doubt from unkind words about my appearance; the body stress response every time I heard my bully's name; the spiralling into fear every time my phone rang at night because my bully would call me after hours. Unlearning is hard.

When I was at school, I had a negative experience with a maths teacher who left me feeling stupid and deflated. He would single me out in a class full of talking students, berate me if I didn't know the answer and roll his eyes if I asked a question for clarity. Maths became my worst subject, and I hated going into his class. I remember wanting to quit learning because he made me feel extremely uncomfortable.

After multiple incidents, my mother questioned the issue, and the teacher told my mother we had a personality clash and he didn't like me. It's bizarre to think that a teacher could openly admit to disliking a 14-year-old girl to her mother. It knocked my confidence, especially when he told me I wouldn't amount to much in my career and future.

When I was moved out of his class, I flourished. My new teacher mentored, supported and coached me. I went from failing the subject to passing with a B as my final grade, which I was happy about and worked hard to get. But my previous teacher's words sourly impacted my confidence, especially around maths, equations and numbers. It wasn't until I started my business that I had to expend effort to consciously unlearn my fear around numbers. Every time my accountant would question my figures, I would freeze, get hot and sweaty, and feel incompetent. Over time, and after finding an accountant I trust and and explaining my freeze response, I have learned to love numbers and feel comfortable talking about them.

James Clear says in his book *Atomic Habits* that small changes are the key. I always ask my clients to be 1 per cent better each day a week. Chunking down the unlearning can make it easier and not so overwhelming.

Exercise: Unlearning programmed fear

Can you think of a time in your life when someone made a negative impact on you? What might you need to unlearn? Their words? Their negative energy?

Tall poppy syndrome

I have learned about tall poppy syndrome since being in Australia and observed that it penetrates both workplaces and schools. Tall poppy syndrome is the belief that a person who stands higher than the rest (for example, because of social class, financial status, academic achievements or sporting achievements) should be cut down to size so as not to create an imbalance in the field or attract unfair attention compared to others. The term is used to mask immature and unfair responses to jealousy, most commonly in the workplaces or schools.

Employees feel the need to both shine in front of their employer and also demonstrate teamwork. These needs can often contradict each other, causing stress and unrest between colleagues. The office should be a place for workers to thrive and make improvements. There needs to be awareness of how leaders can encourage others to grow into tall, thriving poppies. While it is outwardly encouraged, many leaders feel that it is necessary to prevent this growth as it threatens their other employees and may draw unwanted attention.

With Australia valuing teamwork so highly, it seems both fitting and contradictory that tall poppy syndrome is so prominent in the Australian workplace. On the one hand, we should uplift one another and allow each other to grow and flourish; but on the other hand, if one of us shines brightly, does that make the rest of us seem lesser or lazy? This is a common thought process that we need to combat. One person's success does not define another person's failure. We achieve different successes and overcome different failures at different times in our career. Likewise, blowing someone else's candle out does not make yours burn any brighter.

I've noticed, having worked both in the UK and Australia, that Australia's tall poppy syndrome is extremely prominent. Simply working too hard can attract negative comments from colleagues. For example, when I started winning awards for my culture-based work, my bully increased his bullying behaviour. He was especially disgruntled when I was nominated for the Northern Territory Young Achiever of the Year award.

There is a common acceptance of toxicity in the workplace as a result of this poppy-cutting behaviour. It deters people from reaching their career goals for fear of being put down or hated. Notions of trust, enthusiasm and productivity all go out the door. A study carried out by Dr Rumeet Billan, Thomson Reuters and Women of Influence found that, out of 1501 participants from various organisations and workplaces, 87.3 per cent felt their successes had been discounted and undermined by fellow employees and leaders, and 81 per cent felt they had experienced hostility or were penalised because of their success.

How can leaders be so highly focused on innovation and improvement in the workplace while also avoiding the toxic nature of tall poppy syndrome? How can we grow out of this trend? Here are some tactics:

- Actively celebrate others' successes and encourage growth within your team, whether you are the leader or a peer. It's how teams thrive. You will then find yourself thriving too.
- Understand that another's success does not define your failure. The absence of success and opportunity does not equate to failure and dead ends. Our career trajectories do not only travel upwards, and we reach different goals at different stages. The comparison of success only harms our confidence in our own ability while creating an overly competitive environment focused on individual gain as opposed to the organisation's goals. I like to tell my clients, 'The only person you should be in competition with is the person you were yesterday'.
- Lead your team towards a common goal and work cohesively. The goal is not who can achieve the plan the quickest but how we can achieve our goals as a team.

Exercise: Learning to unlearn

Think about the behaviours, habits and mindset you need to unlearn, and focus on what you need to learn and change. What needs the most attention? What are you not doing?

Chapter 10

Lead

This chapter is about walking the talk. As Mahatma Gandhi said, 'You must be the change you want to see in the world'.

As a leader, you know by now that your true power lies in your ability to empower those around you. It is your influence that makes the magic happen and sets collective movements in motion. Leadership has nothing to do with your position in the company; it has everything to do with your desire to share a vision of excellence and how you lead by demonstration. It's about your influence, not your authority. As a leader, your well-directed words and actions can inspire and create change. Your values are your best qualities.

Everyone has the power to influence change, create a vision for a better and more inclusive future, and cultivate individual and team values to fundamentally shift workplace culture.

When I think of an upstander leader, I don't picture some silver-headed politician or boardroom executive, or someone in a well-tailored suit in a glass office in a big bank, or any of my previous managers – although any of them could be upstander leaders. What I imagine is someone who hasn't got a traditional hierarchical position or a job title as a leader or manager. I picture the spark, passion and fire within a person, regardless of the job title or status.

Here are some examples:

- Ben, who is a frontline worker, completed my Upstander Leader Masterclass and started challenging his crew's behaviours and toxic banter.
- Roselyn, who works in a library, had the courage to break up a fight outside her workplace and de-escalate the situation.
- Hannah, who works at a childcare centre, decided to take a stance against worker gossip by outlining how it was causing team tensions that needed to be resolved.
- Justin, who works at an airport, realised that not only was he on the edge of burnout, but also his team was at risk of harm. He called out the toxic culture of overworking and lack of personal boundaries, and took a stand to change the conditions.
- Laura, who works in finance, did not like how a senior manager was speaking down to her and her team. She used her voice to boldly and courageously tell the person that she didn't appreciate being humiliated in public forums and would appreciate a behaviour change. The negative behaviour stopped.

You, as a leader, can impact your whole team and organisation by being an upstander and supporting other upstander leaders like those above.

In this chapter, we will explore why influence is more important than authority, how to find your first followers, and about the importance of being willing to be the first follower and having a clear vision for change.

Influence over authority

Leadership is about influence, and you don't need a specific title to have influence. It is also about caring for human beings, capturing hearts and minds, and inspiring others to come up with ideas and share experiences. To better your workplace climate, and to be future-focused, the old model of authority rules must go – it doesn't work for future-focused workplaces, especially if bullying is enshrined as leadership.

Take former US President Donald Trump as an example. It's widely documented that he operated as a bully, sacking everyone who didn't agree with him. That didn't last. What do you replace authority with? Influence. The upstander effect is about influence – showing people the way, calling out bad behaviours and developing better alternatives. Leaders have many tools they can use to assert their influence – such as casual encounters from 'management by walking around' (as my business coach Nigel would say), presentations at meetings, mentoring and coaching, and even learning programs.

Leaders influence when they reach people in ways that help them to understand and inspire them to act. Influence is about proactively changing ideas and behaviours. It is one of the key leadership skills to build team synergy and rally people around your vision and purpose.

Change doesn't have to be top-down. Once you understand that you can have influence without authority, this is when the change occurs. In 2021, I was working with David Waddell, CEO of Orange City Council. During a ceremony at the end of my work there, the council's workforce shared that the biggest impact of the Upstander movement for them was the fundamental shift in their leaders' trust and communication. It had moved from a typical top-heavy decision-making structure to an innovative culture where influence and ideas were generated at the frontline level.

The middle management team of 120 leaders built their skills and graduated to upstander leaders over a period of several months. In the workshops, directors and frontline supervisors were all part of the same activities, working in collaboration and learning from each other – in many cases for the first time. In one workshop, I heard a conversation in which Lynn, who works in customer service, thanked David for the chance to give honest feedback to decision-makers on what they had seen in the workplace and how it could be improved. A personal win for me was when a senior leader reached out to me for one-on-one coaching on how to create an upstander culture and drive the movement forward. He realised he wanted to move from his own task-driven approach to develop his upstander relationship skills.

Exercise: Where are you on the influence versus authority scale?

Ask yourself, 'How frequently do I get feedback – good or bad – directly from my team?' Once a day? Once a week? Once a month? Once a year? Never?

When I coach leaders, they often scrunch up their face when I mention feedback, especially from direct reports. From experience, it doesn't happen often – or even at all. Feedback can be uncomfortable, but it is an essential tool for upstander leaders.

Enrolling first followers

Being an upstander leader isn't always easy. It can be difficult to get people to buy in. Building buy-in is a skill that comes more naturally to some than others. The good news is it can be learned and mastered by anyone. The first step in developing an upstander culture is to get just one person to follow your lead in upstander behaviour. This is what is known as a 'first follower', 'cultural ally' or even 'upstander champion'. Whether the idea you are bringing is big or small, having a first follower can be the difference between standing alone and getting full buy-in from those you are leading.

It's important to get that first follower and light the spark that ignites your vision. The first follower will take you from standing alone to becoming an upstander leader with a team, creating change.

First Follower: Leadership Lessons from Dancing Guy is a YouTube video with 7 million views. The video is shot at a music festival. A lone guy gets up to dance on a hill, and everyone just stares. Then one guy follows suit, and suddenly more and more people join. That is how a movement is started. When creating an upstander culture and championing change, you can feel like a loner on a hill, but adding just one other person can transform your idea into a movement.

In 2014, during my time in Darwin, I was asked to help make up the numbers at a culture program in my workplace. They didn't really value workplace culture at the time. I remember it being just part of a tick-the-box exercise that the client was requiring, but I'm always a keen learner, so I took the opportunity. The two-hour training session shifted something inside me. I became the first follower of what would eventually be a workplace culture program that I would lead in the organisation.

Over time, I won a slew of awards for my work in this program. Looking back, that one workshop fundamentally shifted my internal compass. The workshop was about leading culture change by being a culture action team member. Hearing the leader's vision of creating a safe, productive environment that people would leave injury-free was articulated in such a way that I emotionally bought in, realising that this was fundamental for the success of our company.

Exercise: Articulating your vision

Think about how you articulate your vision. Do you articulate it in such a way that your team understands that it has value and is worth them buying in to?

As part of the Upstander Leader Masterclass Series, I co-delivered a masterclass called 'The Power of Influence and Collaboration' in partnership with subject-matter expert Natalie Welch, in which we explained the significant influence of the first follower. Being a first follower is an underappreciated form of leadership. It's about building the Upstander movement by moving from 'me' to 'we' principles.

Take the leap of courage to move from a one-man band to a movement. Who will be your first follower? Give your first followers key roles in helping you take the next step, such as generating ideas on how to create cultural change. Start small and ask your team for input. Tweak your vision and cultural movement based on feedback. What do people need? What do people want? What needs to change? Lead valuable, open and honest conversations. Make sure you're encouraging diversity, not groupthink. Don't over-rely on your first followers or go-to team member; explore how you can enrol other followers into your vision. Always using the same champions can backfire and be perceived as favouritism. It also doesn't allow diversity of thought.

Leave your ego out

Upstander leaders are willing to let others take the lead. They are not frightened by other people's skills and competencies. They are not threatened by members of their team taking the lead on change – in fact, they welcome it. They know that when the team is leading change, it makes things easier, but it also involves being willing to be the first follower from time to time. There is nothing worse than a leader who takes all the credit for the team's efforts and discredits others' ideas. Leading with ego and believing that it is your way or the highway will get in the way of deeper connections. This is the definition of authority, not influence.

Share the load. Less will land on your desk, and you can sleep easier at night. I've seen people become toxic when they are slapped with a leadership title and their ego takes hold of them. Leadership is about removing ego.

Reflecting on my own workplace bullying experience, my bully led with his ego. Winning awards and having my competency celebrated infuriated him. His ego led him to believe that he should be the best, and that by doing well I was showing him up – a classic case of tall poppy syndrome. If people challenged his decisions, they didn't last long in the job.

Exercise: Ego no-go

Take a long, hard look in the mirror. Are you leading with others' best interests at heart, or are you driven by your own ego and success – more competition than collaboration? In recent months, how often have you given your appreciation to and celebrated your team? Once a day? Once a week? Once a month? Once in a blue moon? Never?

Have a clear vision for change

No one wants to follow a leader who doesn't have reason for leadership and influence. Inspire confidence in yourself and those around you by coming up with a vision that aligns with your values and your purpose, and articulate it whenever necessary to keep everyone on track. Everyone is more passionate about their work when they follow someone who has a clear vision.

Your vision is how you will carry out your purpose, why you're doing what you're doing. For example, my vision is to build a generation of upstanders – one person, one voice, and one action at a time. My purpose is to stop human and workplace suffering.

To be a successful upstander leader, you need to have a clear vision so you are easy to follow. Having a clear vision means you can easily articulate it, and enrol your upstander allies and your first followers.

Establishing a clear vision in a team and organisation is the key to gaining support and creating change. A statement of vision says, 'Here's the direction we will take, here's where we are going in the future, and here's how we're going to change the world'. Each year, I sit down with my team during planning day and put the company vision at the front of our minds. As we move through the session and make critical strategy decisions, I constantly say, 'Does this align with our vision?' Throughout the year, opportunities and new partners present themselves. Each time, I reflect on whether they add value and align with my vision, or hinder it and sway it off course into uncharted waters.

As an entrepreneur, it's important for me to do this. In the past, like many other entrepreneurs and business owners, I have fallen victim to shiny object syndrome: when new opportunities come along, I have jumped in feet first and not taken a moment to ensure the opportunity is aligned to my vision. If you want to lead people to a specific destination, you need to have a clear vision of how you want to get there and get your team on board to achieve it.

An upstander leader's vision must be ingrained in the culture and be ambitious, articulate and exciting. The vision inspires buy-in and is a critical asset for leaders to drive high performance. It infuses the workplace and affects every employee who is engaged in living this set of actions, beliefs, values and goals. They want to share your vision.

Here are some examples of vision statements:

- Canva: 'To empower everyone in the world to design anything and publish anywhere'

- Atlassian: 'To help unleash the potential of every team'
- Harley-Davidson: 'We fulfil dreams through the experiences of motorcycling'
- Disney: 'To entertain, inspire and inform people around the globe'

These are short, aspirational and easy to remember. Successful visions should be hopeful and positive, clear and concise, inspiring and energising. They should be capable of guiding decision-making and the allocation of resources, and creating consistency in teams and organisations.

You can have a personal vision statement, but I wouldn't recommend crafting company vision statements solely at the senior management level. I've seen this many times, when senior leaders decide the vision and email it across the company. Big no-no. Culture needs to be the sum of everyone.

Exercise: Write to your future upstander-leader self

Write a one- or two-paragraph letter to yourself. Imagine you are your future self, an upstander leader, and advise your current self how you got there. Articulate your vision. How would you communicate it? How would you enrol your team? How would you enrol your first follower?

Personal values

In 2021 I interviewed Michele Danno on the Jessica Hickman Podcast, and she told me about her experience interning at one of the big entertainment media outlets in the US. Michele values inclusion, diversity and equality, and on her first day as an intern she received a clear indication that the company had very conflicting values to hers:

'One group was the studio interns – this was for a large entertainment media station – and the studio interns were all non-white students. It felt like anyone who didn't fit the typical face of media was put into the studio because they would be behind the scenes. And then the marketing event interns, they all looked like me. They were all white, conventionally "attractive"…

'…And when the internship coordinator hosted the orientation, she told us, "OK, first and foremost, I just have to say the number-one rule here is there will be no fraternising within the organisation, because we've had issues in the past of interns getting involved with talent." And I'm like, OK, here we go – first thing off the mark is that there's a workplace hook-up culture. Great. Then she was like, "We had over 2500 applicants, but, if you look around, you'll notice that everyone in this room was chosen for a reason – you all reflect the image we're trying to project. You'll be going to a lot of events together, so you may be tempted…"

'Aside from the many reasons this is discriminatory, ableist and problematic for those who don't fit the media mould, I also felt somewhat disheartened by her comments, even though I apparently did "look the part". I was pursuing multiple majors in relevant areas of study and had nearly perfect grades, so academically I should have qualified. I also had a lot of relevant work experience in similar roles at my university, and I just felt like, what? Was I chosen for my capabilities and my potential, or because I am blonde and thin and white? What happens when I age, or if I have an accident, or gain weight?

Is the working world only going to accept me or advocate for me if I look how they want?

'... Then there was a girl next to me – this was so awkward – and she was heavier than the rest of us. And I'll never forget, she leaned over and was just like, "Wow. Well, I had a phone interview. That explains a lot."

'No one wins in an organisation that makes everyone feel either self-doubty or disposable. Looks are so subjective, fleeting and tenuous – not a secure foundation on which to build a career. I was 19 and this had been my dream employer. I hadn't even started yet, but I already knew I couldn't work there long-term. It was a fun summer, but I never pursued employment after the three months.'

Walk away from work that undermines your personal values. It may seem obvious what values are, but how you apply them in your daily life isn't always so clear. Many people who I coach aren't sure what they value and how those values affect the decisions they make or define them as individuals. Personal values are the things you deem important to you and that you consider integral in your decision-making. However, it is easy to find yourself ignoring these and making snap decisions for quick gains.

Everyone has their own individual values. Your values may not align with others', and that's okay. You may also feel differently about how you abide by your values: some people would prefer that every decision they make reflects their values, whereas others feel that's only necessary for major decisions.

For example, I may choose to live a more environmentally friendly lifestyle by recycling and watching my waste, and I may hold this as an important value, yet still find myself using single-use plastic straws from time to time. But for my friend, this might be a big no-no – they might make the decision to request either no straw or a more environmentally friendly one. A value of yours may be to only purchase local, organic produce; others may not value this as highly. Everyone differs in the extent to which they feel they must hold true to their values. Respect that and ensure that your big decisions – such as where you work, the people you build relationships with and the political stand you take – reflect your own personal values.

If you don't understand what your values are, it can be hard to develop your upstander leadership. You can often find yourself feeling guilty for unknown reasons because you've unconsciously made decisions or allowed actions that go against your values.

Earlier in the book, we talked about the importance of empathy, ethics and equality. These guide you to think about values. Living by your personal values means identifying your non-negotiables. One of my non-negotiable values is freedom. Having freedom to express my truth and be my authentic self is highly important to me. When I worked in a toxic workplace, having this freedom limited caused me internal conflict and unhappiness. To give you another example, I once worked with a client who worked in coal mining but who was passionate about climate change and environmentally friendly resources. They felt there was an internal values conflict in their role, which caused them unhappiness and unfulfilment. They later got a job working in renewable energy resources.

Earlier, I talked about when I entered a consulting partnership that didn't work out. Our values were misaligned. I've sometimes entered into partnerships with people who had different values to me. For example, I value collaboration and making sure that serving the humans comes first and money comes later, but some people strongly believe in profit over people. This has led to some really toxic behaviours that, on reflection, definitely misaligned with my values. I also value personal development and growth, while others may not.

Exercise: Identifying your values

Answer the following questions carefully – you may find value in something you've never considered before:

- What is important to you in your work, social and personal life?
- How does your career support or go against your values?
- What problems bother you?
- In what areas of your personal life and relationships do you find yourself encountering issues?
- What do you find yourself disagreeing with your colleagues and friends over?
- What makes you proud?
- When are you happiest?
- How do you think you can make the world a better place?
- What makes you feel disappointed in your personal life or in society?
- What attributes do you want to be remembered for?

Write down the top 10 things that appear most often in your answers; these are likely to be your values. For example, mine are health, love, family, kindness, empathy, relationships, freedom, equality, respect and ethics.

It isn't always easy to live by your values. We often make decisions subconsciously. Work on aligning your lifestyle choices with your values, and lead by example. Begin by making your decision-making a conscious act – at least for your bigger decisions.

Here's how you can make your decisions a conscious act:

- Make a habit of updating your values list as you learn and grow. Each time you read it, you'll be reminded of your values.

- Visualise your everyday routines and think about how you can alter them to support or express your values.
- Make a little poster of your values. Use the poster to make visual cues that gently remind you of what is important to you.
- Reflect upon past decisions that did not feel aligned with your values and analyse why you might have made them. Don't dwell on this – reflect positively and constructively.

Team values

When I ask leaders and organisations what their personal versus company values are, they're often unable to answer. The core values of a team are what bring people together to thrive and work productively with enthusiasm and discipline. So, how can a large group of people with different values work together towards a common goal? They must define common and core values as a team, accept and respect differences within the team, and determine what they are and aren't prepared to sacrifice with regard to their own values.

We have spoken about the importance of understanding and defining your own values, but integrating them into life and work is far more complex. It requires consistent and conscious effort, particularly in group settings, where differences in action and thought are going to occur. You want your company's culture to be developed around a core set of values that all workers respect and adhere to. You do not want culture to be developed by randomly mixing employee values and company culture. Pre-emptive, conscious and meaningful choices are needed.

Team values and company culture have an external impact as well as an internal one. Consumers appreciate companies that offer a product or service that is consistent with their values and culture. It shows that the product has had thought put into it.

While building my business, I created some values that were important to my work and mission. When onboarding team members and business partners, I ensure I articulate those values to check for alignment. I also ask for a copy of their personal values (and for business partners, their company values).

My business values are:

- to be humanistic – connecting hearts, minds and individual ideas and experiences
- to be holistic – a whole-person, whole-team and whole-organisation approach
- to be synergistic – working together for collective success
- to be futuristic – building an upstander generation now for the future of work.

When I work with clients, I ensure that they have a copy of my values pre-engagement to make sure we're a good fit and create a strong principled partnership.

In 2021, I helped an executive team in a government organisation unpack how they would like to lead, and what values they would like to uphold and cultivate across the team and organisation. This was a reminder that even some of the most established organisations in Australia need to put some work into defining their values, which is a fundamental step in creating an upstander culture.

How can you develop team values? Asking yourself the questions in the previous exercise and coming to an understanding of your own values will give you a basic guide on how to set and develop team values – but exactly how can your team achieve these steps?

The organisation must have a solid idea of what it stands for before employing workers. This will allow for an easier development of common values. People – millennials and gen Z in particular – want to know the values and the cultural expectations of the workplace before they join.

The values developed by an organisation need to be strong, specific and sustainable, and should be kept in mind when hiring employees. Once the team is built upon the same values and cultural expectations, it is time to develop behaviours that reflect these values. This is when accepting and representing differences is important. There is more than one way to create an ethical, sustainable product.

As well as actively supporting and encouraging diversity, begin by implementing policies within the workplace that prohibit discrimination of any sort. Provide courses or other informational resources to allow employees to learn about and understand diversity, empathy, ethics and equality. Explore what prejudices your team members have learned through ignorance and lack of awareness and education. Encourage respectful discussions about differences of opinion. Acknowledge that all employee values and ideas are equal.

Fair compromises in creating common values and culture are important. It's important to start seeing compromise as a strong aspect of your team culture and not a weak one. Acceptance of diversity and enthusiasm will help you to reach a common goal. All parties must learn to compromise, not just a few. We need to be able to discuss ideas openly, express concerns and reach compromises to create an open, honest, upstanding culture.

Chapter 11

Love

In this chapter, we're going to explore how step five, love, is fundamental to an upstander leader's toolkit. Love is what animates all the other steps to becoming an upstander and makes them meaningful.

Let me clarify before you tense up and think, 'Love? In a leadership book?' I'm not talking about romantic love. I'm talking about compassionate love – warmth, kindness, connection, sentiment – which leads to caring leaders and caring humans. A lot of leadership books talk about 'care', so the word 'love' might feel slightly foreign. Love, kindness and inner knowledge have led me to share my work and be a passionate advocate for change. In this chapter, we will explore why 'love' isn't an icky word that needs to be locked away at work.

Love must be at the core of our workplaces. It's important to value love for ourselves, love for others, love for our environment and community, and love for life itself. With more love in the world, we can create movements, inspire peace and empower people to engage, show up and bring their whole selves to every conversation.

Many people compromise love and kindness by working in toxic environments. They think they can't change. But love is a basic need. Upstander leaders have a solid understanding of human needs, and enough awareness to be able to assess how those needs should be met in a work environment.

According to Maslow's hierarchy of needs, our most basic needs are physiological – food, water, air, shelter and sleep. Take any of these away and we stop functioning. That's why many people felt stressed during the pandemic when their basic human needs were being challenged. Fear of a lack of food led to panic-buying, and super-markets were unable to keep up with increased demand, which led to more fear. People were also affected by increased adrenaline, causing lack of sleep, which inhibited their ability to function normally.

Once these primary needs are met, however, we have a whole list of other needs for things that make our lives worth living. These start with the feeling of safety and security, and then the sense of belong-ing. (These were also impacted by the pandemic – people's safety and security were threatened by the health risks and job insecurity, and their sense of belonging was impacted by the lockdowns preventing face-to-face contact with friends and family.) That becomes the basis for self-esteem, which then evolves into a yearning to reach our full potential.

When these needs aren't being met, it doesn't take long for cracks to start appearing in our wellbeing. Throughout this book, I've talked about creating a sense of safety from bullying and toxic behaviours. As soon as those behaviours disappear, your team will start to feel a sense of belonging and love that will flourish naturally, as long as you encourage it.

I know this because I worked in a toxic work environment. My ego replaced compassionate love, and kindness was a no-show. For years, I hid away my authentic self to fit into a toxic, masculine culture where love was hidden, abolished, unrecognisable. But love is our deepest craving. What humans crave most of all is love and belonging – everyone deserves the right to experience compassionate love, respect and kindness.

Employees who consistently feel loved, valued and appreciated by their employers are far more likely to put in significant effort on the organisation's behalf. A survey of more than 1700 adults by the American Psychological Association found that 'employees who feel valued are more likely to report better physical and mental health, as well as higher levels of engagement, satisfaction and motivation compared to those who do not feel valued by their employers'. Feeling valued is one of those aspects of belonging that leads to a sense of love.

Leaders need love. So, how can we incorporate love into the workplace and leadership?

Leaders need love

Love is about doing what you love with the people you love. Humans want to be loved. I have the privilege of working with leaders across different industries, and I have found that loneliness is common. It makes leadership so hard. People often get promoted because they are extremely good at their specialty or are subject-matter experts, but when they make the jump to leadership, they no longer feel that they are part of the team or experience peer support, regular conversations, feedback and banter. There is often an invisible glass box around the leader. They feel they need to know all the answers, embarrassed if they have to ask for help, and like they should always have their shit together. They carry the problems of the workforce.

Leaders feel insecure when competing priorities arise from above and below. This can lead to burnout, fatigue and loss of confidence in themselves, their role and the people around them. This can cause grumpy, unrecognisable, unapproachable leaders, and so the vicious circle continues. They get stuck in a rut.

When I reconnected with leaders to do workshops in person after having to work online during the COVID-19 pandemic, everyone was so happy to see one another and connect. Leaders need peer support and to understand they don't need to be isolated. They can learn to be more honest about their needs and their role.

Whenever I get to work with organisations, I love to ask, 'Who's asking the leaders if they're okay? Have you asked your leader if they're okay?' Irrespective of your job title, everyone needs to feel a sense of love and belonging. Meeting human needs is as critical in a work environment as in any other part of life. All too often, when I ask a leader how they are, they're surprised. Leaders' need for a sense of love and belonging is forgotten.

Our work helps us find who we are and who we aspire to be. Our need to reach our highest potential can be satisfied by finding true meaning in our job. But our need to belong can either be nurtured or ignored by the organisation's culture. Our self-esteem is impacted by how we are accepted, loved and acknowledged by our peers, our organisation and our industry.

An upstander leader is never dismissive of their colleagues' needs. They're grateful for what they have. They're grounded in reality, authentic, purposeful and principled. They believe that when just one person feels left out in the workplace, it erodes engagement and productivity. They know that facilitating recognition, trust and respect helps everyone.

The power of this idea has allowed me to have some deep conversations with leaders who felt terribly lonely. Even big, strapping lads on construction sites have ended up in tears. A *Harvard Business Review* article by Sigal Barsade and Olivia A O'Neill states, 'In organizations where employees felt and expressed companionate love toward one another, people reported greater job satisfaction, commitment, and personal accountability for work performance'. Love is not a word you hear often in office hallways or conference rooms, and yet it has a strong influence on workplace outcomes. The more love core workers feel, the more engaged they are.

So, what does a culture of compassionate love look like? Imagine a pair of co-workers collaborating side by side each day, expressing care and consideration towards one another, safeguarding each other's feelings, and showing tenderness and compassion when things don't go well. Now imagine a workplace that encourages those behaviours from everyone – where managers actively look for ways to create and reinforce close working relationships amongst employees.

In 2020, I was running a workshop in which a lady was unpacking the concept of love at a table with her co-workers. She openly shared a story with the room: 'Love is so important. This morning while driving to this workshop, I asked Siri to text my daughter. Siri misinterpreted what I said and sent the text, "I love you." My daughter instantly called me and said, "What is wrong? Why did you text me this?"' Laughing, the lady said, 'Nothing's wrong. Why would you say that?' Her daughter replied that she never texted her 'I love you'. The woman shared with the room that of course she loved her children, but she realised the simple phrase 'I love you' was underused.

I'm not telling you to say 'I love you' to your colleagues – that's not appropriate for the workplace – but to stop and think about if your actions and words are loving and kind, or if you need to tell someone you care about that you appreciate them.

What could you do to create compassionate love at work? This matters to you and your team. Encourage love by creating a welcoming and inclusive environment that leaves people feeling that both their presence and efforts are respected, acknowledged and appreciated. To show gratitude is to show love. Public appreciation is a great way to recognise and reward employees, and so are private expressions of gratitude and appreciation.

Give your time and listen to colleagues and employees. This will show them that you see them, care for them and have concern for them. Lend a hand to people when you can.

LOVE: Living Our Values Everyday

If the word 'love' still makes you feel icky, here's another way to look at it: 'Love' is an acronym of Living Our Values Everyday. (I know some of you detail-oriented people will probably be thinking 'every day' should be two words, but for ease of remembering this simple acronym we will join them – much to my editor's despair!) In chapter 6, I talked about how empathy, ethics and equality are the values upstander leaders need to embody. If you want to feel more comfortable talking about love in the workplace, explore how it can become a value of yours.

In 2019, I interviewed Andrew on my podcast. Andrew was proud to discuss the role of love in his values as a people leader. As a managing director working at one of the top 10 retailers internationally, he successfully managed a multi-billion-dollar operation responsible for 1900 staff across 74 locations. He did all this while achieving work-life balance: he had been happily married for 15 years and was a loving father who loved to travel, scuba dive and be in nature.

Andrew discussed the power and importance of knowing your values – and not just knowing them, but understanding them as a priority. He said once you understand those values, you can connect with your people on a different level. He also said that it's important to understand whether these are your values or someone else's values that have been imprinted on you. In some cases, values can be imprinted from parents. He said that when thinks about his life and the things that have led him to now, he often reflects that he could have had someone else's values. He would have loved to tell his younger self, 'Hey, look at your values. What serves you? What is going to be really important to you in your life and career? Understand it and then live by your values. Once you really know your values and what you value deeply, it can set you up for success.'

Andrew also told me that his number-one value is love. He thought about every decision that he made, and every decision was made with absolute clarity because he was 100 per cent in alignment with his values. His number-two value is health, and he said that this was fundamental in his decision-making. It also took many decisions off the table. He would tell his younger self that everything he does needs to be in alignment with what he wants in his life. 'It's not easy, but having strong values gives you a clear ability to make decisions.'

Building on the value of love, Andrew discussed his role of heart-centred leadership: 'I think the big thing for heart-centred leadership, or what I see as the major thing, is what it takes to lead from love'. He said that people often have misconceptions about the word 'love' and assume it's romantic or a fairytale, but that love comes down to a basic concept of compassion, respect and kindness for other people. If you are leading with love, then no matter when you need to take action, make decisions, move your organisation forward or overcome challenges and obstacles, you will still fundamentally love and treat your people with respect, compassion and kindness – because you see them for who they truly are.

Andrew said he'd had a number of people say to him, 'I can't believe you're talking about love in this modern business era'. He gave me a good example of a situation in which he needed to perfor-mance-manage someone:

'If I'm needing to manage someone's performance, I can still do that with love. I can still see the situation for what it is. I can still review everything with openness, transparency and respect. It might be that, at the end of that, I need to come to a hard decision.

'In some cases, for example, I might have to let someone go from the organisation or deal with a serious matter, but it can still be done with love, and it can be done with respect. I've had people who I've had to do that to, and from that I've had people I've had to cut from the business. They've come back to me later and thanked me for doing it with love and compassion. The difference is respecting and loving the people in a broader sense, not in the narrow and Western romantic sense.'

Exercise: Positioning love as a value

Imagine giving advice to a young leader who has just joined your organisation. How could you position the idea of love as a value? What might you discuss? What might you ask?

The role of love for the upstander leader

Princess Diana said, 'I don't go by the rule book. I lead from the heart, not the head'. Decades after her tragic death, she still inspires me with this quote and her approach to being an upstander on issues and topics that were controversial at the time, such as HIV. Diana epitomises the upstander leader.

Leading with love is not a distant, unachievable dream that only born leaders can do. It's about managing external pressures through your ability to pause and reflect. That's why I love to run my Reflect and Connect workshop. It's about developing the ability to have a self-check-in and self-analysis to ensure the decision, direction and process is fair and ethical.

Upstander leadership is people-centric and always puts the company's biggest asset, the people, first. If you want to adopt an upstander leadership approach, even when you might have to make a tough business decision and have tough conversations, your people will respect, trust and back you. It puts you in a powerful position, which leaves a lasting impact. As Maya Angelou said, 'People will forget what you said, people will forget what you did, but people will never forget how you made them feel'.

In 1996, John Mackey, CEO of Whole Foods Market, stated that the company was a social system, not a hierarchy. 'We don't have lots of rules handed down from headquarters in Austin. We have lots of self-examination going on. Peer pressure substitutes for bureaucracy. Peer pressure enlists loyalties in a way that bureaucracy doesn't.'

If the teams around and below you do not feel comfortable to share information amongst each other, trust will not be developed. Whole Foods Market is revolutionary in how transparent they are, so much so that they're often criticised for being eccentric and risking confidential information being leaked to competitors.

Research into the unique standards at Whole Foods Market uncovered that they provide their employees with intellectual property such as financial information and the comparative salary information of their entire management team. They believe in authentic communication, transparency and fairness as a company. It is essential that the ethic of fairness applies to all key organisation processes, such as hiring, promotion, compensation, discipline and termination. As Mackey said, 'Favouritism and nepotism undermine organisation trust'.

Mackey demonstrates that fear is the opposite of love. When fear permeates an organisation, love cannot flourish. For businesses to retain valuable employees, leaders must instil a culture of love that aids fulfilment of higher purpose and follows through on the mission of the company. When it comes to culture, Whole Foods Market is unique. The company crafted a set of written rules named 'The Declaration of Independence' that works in conjunction with the mission and values of the company. Mackey insists on opening new stores with a few pre-existing staff members to start a culture. Employees who have a thorough understanding of the company and the culture can lay the foundation for new team members.

Other companies adopting a similar mindset include PepsiCo, which lists 'caring' as its guiding principle on its website, and Zappos, which also explicitly focuses on 'caring' as one of its values: 'We are more than a team, though. We are a family. We watch out for each other, care for each other and go above and beyond for each other'.

While 'love' may feel like an icky word to use in your organisation's values and missions, and in a leadership statement, companies are moving in this new direction and instilling love as a value.

Exercise: Instilling love

As an upstander leader, how can you integrate love into your practices and your team culture?

Love starts with self

Before you can love others, especially at work, you need to work on your self-love and your self-care.

'To lead successfully, one must fill their own cup before filling others.' I wrote this in my journal when I was at the edge of burnout. After years of burning the candle at both ends, running a race I couldn't win in a toxic environment and ensuring everyone else was okay before myself, I experienced a crash and burn that damaged my nervous system.

When I talk about love of self in workshops, I get the same response: discomfort. But why is it so hard for us in Western culture to value ourselves?

As I write this chapter, I am putting a reminder in my calendar to read this and be proud of my work. It's a glorious morning in December 2021. I'm waiting for the sun to rise as I tap away on my laptop. It has been a giant year for me, with the most amount of time I've ever spent in lockdown due to the COVID-19 pandemic in Australia. It's been almost three years since I've seen my family in the UK, but I can see light at the end of the tunnel. In the next two weeks, I have some big events, keynotes and workshops – and a book deadline. I haven't even thought about Christmas shopping yet. When I scan back over 2021, I can observe moments when I became a bystander to my own life. That fast-paced expectation of doing more and achieving more left me unconscious – not only physically but mentally at times.

I am forever grateful that my business boomed during the pandemic, which meant more work could be achieved online, but this also blurred the lines between Work Jess and Home Jess. I neglected my self-care and often self-love, working into the small hours. People have spoken about COVID fatigue – a new level of tiredness, a burnout that has come from being locked down and then suddenly opened up, and having to relearn to navigate our way through busy environments. I don't know about you, but for me 2021 was a long but fast, fatiguing but energising year – it was one heck of a ride.

As my own leader, I have found that self-love and nurturing yourself is so important, and I guarantee you don't see enough of this.

Throughout 2020 and 2021, I witnessed more leaders on the edge of burnout than I've ever seen before. In chapter 1, we spoke about the decade of change and disruption, and this could be influencing the burnout. Worker culture is more important than ever, in my opinion. The media is reporting bad behaviours and employees are championing change. In December 2021, Kate Jenkins released a report confirming that one in three people in parliament have been sexually harassed. You have a lot on your plate, but the topic of self-care and self-love is important – you need to manage yourself before you can manage others.

Accepting yourself completely can be difficult and will be an ongoing task as you change and grow as a leader. However, once you've reached a level of acceptance and respect for yourself, you will be able to spread love more naturally and sincerely.

So, how can you practise accepting and loving yourself?

· Celebrate the strengths that you recognise in yourself.
· Understand that the voice of doubt and irrationality is often fuelled by biases or misconceptions that you have unconsciously absorbed from your environment.
· Place yourself in environments that make you feel positive and uplifted.
· Forgive yourself for the opportunities you may have missed and the mistakes you may have made. Concern yourself only with the present and your next immediate step for improving yourself. It's okay to grieve the loss of potential. Some of us didn't excel where we thought we would have and aren't where we think we should be, but that doesn't matter. We can find potential elsewhere. No one is good at just one thing.
· Be charitable – not just with money but with your time and heart, too. Explore your community and see how you can help. You'll start to respect your actions and view yourself more highly. Do selfish good deeds, as some might say.

In order for these steps to work, you must learn to recognise the difference between acceptance and resignation. Accepting that you are burnt out and dissatisfied, and that something has to stop, is not the same as resigning or quitting.

In 2021, I interviewed Philip Donato, the Member of the New South Wales Parliament for Orange. What shone through was his love for his community and his passion for fighting for social justice and mental health. Phil also told me a story about when he first entered parliament and how that made him feel.

> 'So, you walk in, and everyone was heckling. All the government side were heckling me … and then Labor [the Opposition] were heckling them because they had lost a seat. So, I walked into this uproar of noise and people just heckling each other – not so much directed at me but each other. That's why they call it "the bear pit" …

> '…It's not the place to go if you can't take criticism – it's a pretty toxic environment. You've got to be able to have a thick skin…

> '…I think things are slowly changing, but I try and make an effort as a Member of Parliament not to engage in that sort of conduct. I guess as long as you're pretty fair, people recognise you as an upstanding leader in the community – very ethical, will speak your truth and call out bad behaviours.'

Exercise: Giving yourself some friendly advice

When I know I'm being too hard on myself, I pretend I'm talking to a friend or a client. What advice would you give to them? Write some notes while imagining you are giving advice to a friend. What would you say? What talents would you help them appreciate? What good qualities and skills do they have? This self-love exercise will help you focus on your best traits, abilities and talents.

Think about the qualities you love most about yourself. Are you unique? Strong? Lovable? Use 'I am' statements: 'I am honest. I am brave. I am creative'. Now list your positive qualities.

*

Step number five to becoming an upstander leader – to love – seems easy, but it is the most unnatural for many people, especially as you move up through organisational hierarchies. Sometimes people forget to lead with the heart. How can you make love your number-one value?

Hopefully by now you've learned that you need to lead with the heart. To create a loving, nurturing environment, look at what needs to change. Think about the five Ls – look, listen, learn, lead and love – and reflect on how love underpins the rest. In a more loving world, humans can thrive and do their best work.

Conclusion

This book is about how to recognise bystander behaviour in yourself and others, and how to take action to be an upstander instead. It's also about helping you understand what bullying behaviour is and what you need to do to stick up for other people and yourself.

The Upstander movement helps people recognise where they might have become a bystander to toxic behaviour and how damaging that can be to physical, psychological and emotional health. The movement takes you from awareness to action. Being an upstander leader is about reflecting on your current workplace, analysing your own leadership and exploring how to be an outstanding people leader. The upstander leader takes a holistic approach to analyse the external workplace culture and the internal behaviours that shape successful human relationships.

Imagine a world where bullying, harassment and toxic behaviours are a thing of the past. Imagine a world where empathy, ethics and equality are the foundations of every workplace culture. You walk into the office and there's no fear of judgement. You step out of bed every morning knowing that your colleagues and leaders support your best interests. You come home from work every night feeling energised, valued, respected, seen and heard, knowing your work is appreciated and your authentic self is celebrated.

Now imagine leading a team that feels this way. How would they improve your leadership success, your team success and your organisation success? How would it feel when you hang your leadership boots up at the end of your career, knowing that you've left a legacy and a positive impact on the lives of others? In this book, you've heard a lot of stories about great and not so great leaders. You now have the opportunity to draw a line in the sand and create your own leadership legacy from this moment on.

The road map is clear. First, work out where your workplace sits at the moment by reviewing the upstander and bystander zones in chapter 5. Once you know where you sit, set your sights on improvement, moving from bystander to upstander. Implement the upstander effect with the five Ls – look, listen, learn, lead and love. They are your means of joining the Upstander movement. Be the change your workplace and the world need to see.

Here are some principles to follow to become an upstander leader:

1. Be open, honest and truthful every time.
2. Trust your people to do the right thing. Do not micromanage.
3. Articulate your vision. Let your team know you are only as successful as them.
4. Be mindful of the words you speak, and know your words can be painful like bullets or uplifting like fairy floss.
5. Walk the talk. Lead by example and put your team's success before your own. There's no room for ego in the upstander leader.
6. Lead with empathy, ethics and equality, and make love one of your values.
7. Catch yourself when you are in the bystander zone, and make sure you correct your course of action.
8. Be non-judgmental. Never make assumptions without facts.

9. Review your whole self. Take time to reflect on your physical self, your emotional health and your mindset. What needs attention?

10. Have the courage to look in the mirror, accept your flaws and embrace your lessons learned.

11. Be committed to your personal and professional growth, adopting the growth mindset.

12. Know that living is giving. Be generous with your time and energy to mentor, coach and grow others.

13. Make sure you listen before sharing your opinions. Listen as an empty vessel for opportunities.

14. Create and celebrate a feedback culture. Get feedback from the bottom up, not just the top down.

15. Be passionate about creating a more hopeful and inclusive environment.

16. Believe that, with the right support, everyone has the potential to thrive and move from bystander to upstander.

17. Commit to ending human and workplace suffering.

One of the most common obstacles leaders tell me about is getting caught up in the business of everyday work and putting the upstander effect in the too-hard basket. If you ignore the effects of bullying and toxic behaviour, though, you are at risk of destroying the health and wellbeing of employees and yourself, and damaging your reputation. The key to productivity is happy, healthy and valued employees. Overwhelm in your business is solved by the upstander effect.

It's time to pay real attention to your employees. In this book, you have all the tools all you need, but I'm also available to help you implement all these strategies – whether it's through an awareness keynote, a capability-building workshop or a partnership to build an upstander culture road map for your organisation.

My mission is to build a generation of upstanders – one person, one voice and one action at a time – and to leave this world in a better place than I found it. I want to end workplace and human suffering. This book can help you become an upstander leader, and I hope you will join the movement to create a more inclusive, hopeful and loving future for this generation and the next.

About the author

Originally from Wales, Jessica came to Australia in 2013 with a backpack and a dream. Falling in love with the country and people, she eventually became an Australian citizen, overcoming many obstacles along the way.

After a negative workplace experience, Jessica has spent the last decade using her background in human resources, workplace health and safety, coaching and behavioural therapy to guide organisations and individuals on how to create healthier, happier workplaces. Jessica's work focuses on empowering others to own their ability to speak out and become champions of change.

As the founder of Bullyology and the driver of the Upstander movement, Jessica has partnered with many well-known businesses across the public, private and not-for-profit sectors to develop upstander leaders, teams and cultures. She has delivered workshops and keynote addresses in the USA, Canada, Australia, New Zealand and the UK.

Jessica is a Mentor for Regional Development Australia and sits on the judging panel for the Business NSW Awards and Australian Admin Awards.

Acknowledgements

To all the upstander leaders who have supported this book coming into fruition: thank you for always shining a light on the elephant in the room. Thank you for continuing to challenge the status quo, to build a more hopeful and inclusive future for all.

To all the future upstanders, I acknowledge your curiosity, and I hope the journey through these pages leaves you feeling optimistic and drives you to be the upstander leaders you are destined to be.

Thank you to all my clients who have trusted me to develop upstander leaders in their organisations and continue to champion the movement.

Big love to my support crew, who have been fundamental to this book's creation. Natalie Welch, Nigel van Reyk, Rebecca Lewis and Sarah Maxwell, you listened and supported my development of the upstander leader concept.

Kath Walters, your book coaching challenged my writing and stretched my thinking into new dimensions.

Lesley Williams, Eleanor Reader and Will Allen at Major Street Publishing, thank you for believing in the power of upstander leaders, and for your continued support.

Special thanks to my husband Troy, who has been with me every step of the way. I wrote this book while navigating the second postponement of our wedding during the pandemic, and your love and patience has been a blessing.

References

Introduction

R.E. Potter, M.F. Dollard & M.R. Tuckey, *Bullying & harassment in Australian workplaces: results from the Australian Workplace Barometer Project 2014/2015*, November 2016, <safeworkaustralia.gov.au/system/files/documents/1705/bullying-and-harassment-in-australian-workplaces-australian-workplace-barometer-results.pdf>.

'Facing the music: the Sony Music scandal', *Four Corners*, television program, ABC NEWS, 11 October 2021, <abc.net.au/4corners/facing-the-music:-the-sony-music-scandal/13579828>.

'Good practice, good business: eliminating discrimination and harassment you're your workplace', Australian Human Rights Commission, <humanrights.gov.au/sites/default/files/content/info_for_employers/pdf/7_workplace_bullying.pdf>, accessed 20 July 2022.

'Bullies and budgets: how much does workplace bullying cost?', WorkPro, <workpro.com.au/bullies-and-budgets-how-much-does-workplace-bullying-cost>, accessed 20 July 2022.

House of Representatives Standing Committee on Education and Employment, *Workplace bullying: we just want it to stop*, October 2012, Canberra, <aph.gov.au/parliamentary_business/committees/house_of_representatives_committees?url=ee/bullying/report.htm>.

B. Evans, 'Student petitions for addition of "upstander" to dictionary', *Washington Square News*, 18 February 2014, <nyunews.com/2014/02/18/upstander/>.

Chapter 1

'Gartner identifies nine trends for HR leaders that will impact the future of work after the coronavirus pandemic', media release, Gartner, Arlington, Va., 6 May 2020, <gartner.com/en/newsroom/press-releases/2020-05-06-gartner-identifies-nine-trends-for-hr-leaders-that-wi>.

R. Nagjee, 'Success lies in getting everyone on the same page', *Gulf News*, 10 June 2018, <gulfnews.com/business/analysis/success-lies-in-getting-everyone-on-the-same-page-1.2234397>.

E. Hoenigman Meyer, 'What is diversity, inclusion and belonging?', Nasdaq, 21 October 2019, <nasdaq.com/articles/what-is-diversity-inclusion-and-belonging-2019-10-21>.

'ALS ice bucket challenge', ALS Therapy Development Institute, <als.net/ice-bucket-challenge/>, accessed 20 July 2022.

Chapter 2

'Bystander effect', Biology Dictionary, <biologydictionary.net/bystander-effect/>, accessed 20 July 2022.

Chapter 3

A. Bolt, 'End this disgrace and get on with the game of footy', *Herald Sun*, 29 May 2013, <news.com.au/sport/afl/end-this-disgrace-and-get-on-with-the-game-of-footy/news-story/91f75ccb0e8a0dd44e6ddcea645b457b>.

'Adam Goodes full press conference transcript as he addresses racist taunts', *Herald Sun*, 25 May 2013, <heraldsun.com.au/sport/afl/adam-goodes-full-racism-press-conference-transcript/news-story/255a9b49ef91175be4e6d73a8c26a30c>.

Chapter 4

T. Spenziero, 'Generations in the workforce', Excelsior College, 16 April 2020, <excelsior.edu/article/generations-in-the-workforce/>.

'Millennials in the workplace statistics: generational disparities in 2022', TeamStage blog, <teamstage.io/millennials-in-the-workplace-statistics/>, accessed 20 July 2022.

E. Wale, 'The key to millennial happiness in the workplace', Clear Search blog, <clearsearch.com.au/blog/the-key-to-millennial-happiness-in-the-workplace>, accessed 20 July 2022.

Y.N. Harari, *Sapiens: a brief history of humankind*, Harper, New York, 2015.

S. Kurian et al., *Meet the millennials*, KPMG, June 2017, <home.kpmg/content/dam/kpmg/uk/pdf/2017/04/Meet-the-Millennials-Secured.pdf>.

M. Drexler, A. Noble & J. Bryce et al., *From the margins to the mainstream: assessment of the impact investment sector and opportunities to engage mainstream investors*, World Economic Forum, September 2013, <www3.weforum.org/docs/WEF_II_FromMarginsMainstream_Report_2013.pdf>.

S. Landrum, 'Why millennials care about social impact investing', *Forbes*, 4 November 2016, <forbes.com/sites/sarahlandrum/2016/11/04/why-millennials-care-about-social-impact-investing/?sh=44cd588259c0>.

Chapter 5

A.C. Edmondson, *The fearless organisation: creating psychological safety in the workplace for learning, innovation, and growth*, John Wiley & Sons, Hoboken, N.J., 2018.

'Ingroup vs. outgroup unconscious bias', Study.com, 22 February 2018, <study.com/academy/lesson/ingroup-vs-outgroup-unconscious-bias.html>.

'How does sexual harassment affect the workplace?', EVERFI blog, <everfi.com/blog/workplace-training/the-effects-of-sexual-harassment-in-the-workplace/>, accessed 20 July 2022.

C.R. Feldblum & V.A. Lipnic, *Select task force on the study of harassment in the workplace*, U.S. Equal Employment Opportunity Commission, June 2016, <eeoc.gov/select-task-force-study-harassment-workplace>.

E. Levenson, 'A woman on a SEPTA train was sexually assaulted while other riders failed to intervene, authorities say', *CNN*, updated 19 October 2021, <edition.cnn.com/2021/10/18/us/philadelphia-train-rape/index.html>.

Chapter 6

D. Goleman, 'The focused leader', *Harvard Business Review*, December 2013, <hbr.org/2013/12/the-focused-leader>.

C. Andre & M. Velasquez, 'Can ethics be taught?', Markkula Center for Applied Ethics, Santa Clara University, accessed 20 July 2022, <https://www.scu.edu/mcae/publications/iie/v1n1/taught.html>.

Equality Act 2010 (UK)

Jessica Hickman – Bullyology, *Upstander Leader Series – Jo Farrell*, video, YouTube, 26 November 2021, <youtube.com/watch?v=EoZhayTNvQ0>.

Chapter 7

A. Mack & I. Rock, *Inattentional blindness*, MIT Press, Cambridge, Ma., 1998.

Chapter 8

Guide to working with Indigenous Australian staff, Charles Sturt University, accessed 1 August 2022, <csu.edu.au/__data/assets/pdf_file/0006/851415/Working-with-Indigenous-Australian-Staff.pdf>.

S Madsen, *The power of project leadership: 7 keys to help you transform from project manager to project leader*, Kogan Page, 2015.

Mental Health First Aid, <mhfa.com.au/>, accessed 20 July 2020.

Chapter 9

J. Clear, *Atomic habits: tiny changes, remarkable results: an easy and proven way to build good habits and break bad ones*, Avery, New York, 2018.

R. Billan, Ph.D., 'When women achieve: the burden of success', LinkedIn, 16 November 2021, <linkedin.com/pulse/when-women-achieve-burden-success-rumeet-billan-ph-d-/>.

Chapter 10

Derek Sivers, 'First follower: leadership lessons from dancing guy', video, YouTube, 11 February 2010, <youtube.com/watch?v=fW8amMCVAJQ>.

'About Canva: empowering the world to design', Canva, <canva.com/about/>, accessed 20 July 2022.

'Atlassian', work@tech, <workat.tech/company/atlassian>, accessed 20 July 2022.

'Harley-Davidson mission and vision statement analysis', mission-statement.com, <mission-statement.com/harley-davidson/>, accessed 20 July 2022.

'Disney mission and vision statement analysis', mission-statement.com, <mission-statement.com/disney/>, accessed 20 July 2022.

'Episode 14: outnumbered - fighting against gender stereotypes with Michéle Danno', The Jessica Hickman Podcast, podcast, 27 October 2019, <listennotes.com/podcasts/the-jessica/episode-14-outnumbered-cWf0TFGmEKD/>.

Chapter 11

'A guide to the 5 levels of Maslow's Hierarchy of Needs', MasterClass, 8 November 2020, <masterclass.com/articles/a-guide-to-the-5-levels-of-maslows-hierarchy-of-needs#what-are-the-5-levels-of-maslows-hierarchy-of-needs>.

'The American workforce faces compounding pressure: APA's 2021 Work and Well-being Survey results', American Psychological Association, <apa.org/pubs/reports/work-well-being/compounding-pressure-2021>, accessed 20 July 2022.

S. Barsade & O.A. O'Neill, 'Manage your emotional culture', *Harvard Business Review*, January–February 2016, <hbr.org/2016/01/manage-your-emotional-culture>.

'Episode 16: heart centred leadership with Andrew & Susan Tindal', The Jessica Hickman Podcast, podcast, 15 January 2020, <listennotes.com/podcasts/the-jessica/episode-16-heart-centred-CZBe9UKFoyh/>.

C. Fishman, 'Whole Foods Is All Teams', *Fast Company*, 30 April 1996, <fastcompany.com/26671/whole-foods-all-teams>.

References

C. Clifford, 'Whole Foods CEO John Mackey: store managers could be making "well over $100,000" without a college degree', CNBC, 5 November 2020, <cnbc.com/2020/11/05/ceo-john-mackey-on-how-much-you-can-make-working-at-whole-foods.html>.

J. Mackey, 'Creating the high-trust organization', Management Innovation eXchange, 18 March 2020, <managementexchange.com/blog/creating-high-trust-organization>.

K.L. Pearson, 'Whole Foods Market ™ case study: leadership and employee retention', *MBA Student Scholarship*, 8, 17 May 2012, <scholarsarchive.jwu.edu/cgi/viewcontent.cgi?article=1007&context=mba_student>.

'SLC 2019: PepsiCo on how to create a culture of caring', *EHS Today*, 7 November 2019, <ehstoday.com/safety-leadership-conference/article/21920448/slc-2019-pepsico-on-how-to-create-a-culture-of-caring>.

'Zappos 10 core values', Zappos Insights, <zapposinsights.com/about/core-values>, accessed 20 July 2022.

M. Hislop, 'Kate Jenkins review reveals 1 in 3 parliamentary staffers have experienced sexual harassment', Women's Agenda, 30 November 2021, <womensagenda.com.au/latest/kate-jenkins-review-reveals-1-in-3-parliamentary-staffers-have-experienced-sexual-harassment/>.

Jessica Hickman – Bullyology, *Upstander Leader Series – Philip Donato*, video, YouTube, 16 December 2021, <youtube.com/watch?v=tOu82FKH18Y>.

Let's work together to build your leadership success and an upstander culture in your workplace!

What's next?

- **Upstanding keynotes:** From each keynote, you will take away insights on becoming big-picture thinkers. Understanding the upstander effect will also help you and your people develop your own voice for change.

- **Upstander workshops:** These workshops are designed to harness the power of the individual to influence others and nurture upstander skills within organisations. Shared learnings help you become purpose-driven thought leaders that are ready to face the future of work.

- **Upstand consulting:** In our sessions, I will help you identify gaps and opportunities for growth within your team or organisation and how to develop and adopt bespoke workforce solutions. Together, we will turn your desired future into reality and move to an upstander workplace culture.

- **Upstand coaching:** Working with individuals, leaders and teams, we establish goals, objectives and roadblocks to success. Each program encourages sharing skills and knowledge for better problem-solving and decision-making to maximise outcomes. I help you establish and promote a modern mindset and improved wellbeing to help you and your team become true upstanders.

- **The Upstand Academy:** This is an ongoing digital curriculum providing a hybrid learning experience that doesn't stop after this book or a keynote is finished. Through consistent, targeted training and capability building, we can build upstanders who become champions of your workplace success.

Note: A keynote is brilliant for setting the tone and getting a burst of motivation and awareness of key issues going on within the workplace – but building capability is fundamental to your leadership success.

Find out more about how Jessica can work with you or your organisation by visiting www.jesshickman.com or www.bullyology.com.

✉ jessica@jesshickman.com

in linkedin.com/in/jessicazoehickman

f @jessicazoehickman @bullyology

○ @jessicazoehickman @bullyology

Be better with business books

MAJOR STREET

We hope you enjoy reading this book. We'd love you to post a review on social media or your favourite bookseller site. Please include the hashtag #majorstreetpublishing.

Major Street Publishing specialises in business, leadership, personal finance and motivational non-fiction books. If you'd like to receive regular updates about new Major Street books, email info@majorstreet.com.au and ask to be added to our mailing list.

Visit majorstreet.com.au to find out more about our books (print, audio and ebooks) and authors, read reviews and find links to our Your Next Read podcast.

We'd love you to follow us on social media.

in linkedin.com/company/major-street-publishing

f facebook.com/MajorStreetPublishing

instagram.com/majorstreetpublishing

@MajorStreetPub